FIST
PUMP

Guido DiErio with Rick
"The Happenstance"
Marinara

RUNNING PRESS
PHILADELPHIA • LONDON

LEGAL DISCLAIMER

Use of company and product names is not authorized by, associated with, or sponsored by any trademark owner, and is intended for literary effect only. *Fist Pump* is a humor book. Its advice and suggestions are meant to make you laugh and are not meant to be taken seriously. Please, use common sense, and don't be a moron. The authors and publisher disclaim all liability in connection with the use of this book.

© 2010 by Guido DiErio

All rights reserved under the Pan-American and
International Copyright Conventions
Printed in Canada

*This book may not be reproduced in whole or
in part, in any form or by any means, electronic
or mechanical, including photocopying, recording,
or by any information storage and retrieval system
now known or hereafter invented, without written
permission from the publisher.*

9 8 7 6 5 4 3 2 1
Digit on the right indicates the number of this printing

Library of Congress Control Number: 2010926111

ISBN 978-0-7624-4065-8

Book design by Matt Goodman
Edited by Jordana Tusman
Typography: Vitesse

Running Press Book Publishers
2300 Chestnut Street
Philadelphia, PA 19103-4371

Visit us on the web!
www.runningpress.com

Be forewarned that there are only seven possible outcomes that will come out of you reading this book:

1) YOU WILL GET LAID.

2) YOU WILL GET PUNCHED.

3) YOU WILL HAVE A THREESOME WITH TWO GUIDETTE HOTTIES.

4) ROID RAGE.

5) YOU WILL OD ON GHB AND DIE.

6) YOU WILL FIST-PUMP THE NIGHT AWAY AND PASS OUT IN A BACK ALLEY SOMEWHERE.

7) HERPES. SORRY, BRO.

CONTENTS

PART I: A STEP-BY-STEP GUIDE TO FULL-BODY GUIDOFICATION — 26

Welcome to the Jersey Shore. It's our personal pleasure to introduce you to this 130-mile slice of heaven along the Atlantic seaboard, a veritable mecca for Guidos and Guidettes every summer. What makes a Guido or Guidette? That's a very complicated question, to be approached with careful nuance and judiciously applied semantics. So many different facets make up these distinct personality

social structure they maintain, to the activities they engage in, Guidos and Guidettes are the product of (and contributors to) an intricate web of hilarity.

The Jersey Shore itself is an incredible place. Each summer, every fake tan and blowout within a one hundred-mile radius descends upon a string of beach communities with the fervor of locusts in biblical times. You may ask, why New Jersey? Well, it's simple, really. New Jersey has become the de facto epicenter for all things Guido, attracting the party-centric from a wide variety of states like New York, Massachusetts, Connecticut, Rhode Island, and New Jersey itself. Hell, some of the 400 people who live in Delaware who aren't related to Joe Biden even make it up to the Shore on an

traits that it's necessary to look at them on a step-by-step basis. From the way these impressive creatures present themselves, to the tightly packed

annual basis. Regardless, this central location and proximity to prime coastal land, and a nightclub scene where very few laws of the United States of America are actually enforced, have conspired

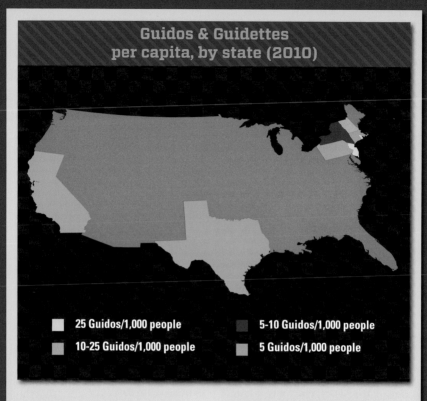

Guidos & Guidettes
per capita, by state (2010)

- ■ 25 Guidos/1,000 people
- ■ 10-25 Guidos/1,000 people
- ■ 5-10 Guidos/1,000 people
- ■ 5 Guidos/1,000 people

to create an incredibly popular tourist destination that has been remarkable in its sustainability. At the end of 2009, New Jersey had taken a commanding lead in Guidos and Guidettes per capita, which triggered several stipulations that will give the state increased access to federal stimulus funds.

This influx of seething testosterone and estrogen needs a place to call home, albeit temporarily. Typically every summer, groups of friends (and even those lucky souls who have not been molested as a by-product of Craigslist personals) will enter into agreements to live together in time-shares with fantastic access to the

beachfront. What soon follows is a testament to excess in terms of love, laughter, and, of course, Jägerbombs. During the peak season of summer shares on the Jersey Shore, approximately 32 percent of all STDs present in North America can be found within a twenty-five-mile radius of Seaside Heights. This includes standard derivations of herpes, syphilis, gonorrhea, and seventeen additional unidentified viral strains that are currently being analyzed by a consortium of the Center for Disease Control, NASA, and representatives from the *Girls Gone Wild* franchise. If you're still having trouble picturing this hedonistic

excess, imagine it's some sort of cross between a Sandals all-inclusive resort and the rubber-extrusion plant off Route 47.

In this setting, characters are plentiful. For every bright-eyed, bushy-tailed youngster eager to make the most of his or her first time at the Shore, there's a seasoned veteran who knows which clubs mix the stiffest drinks and where to buy a pack of Pall Malls at four thirty in the morning. In fact, some people return to the Shore year after year after year, similar to the Wooderson character in *Dazed and Confused*. Really, it's a graceful waltz between machismo and social Darwinism. From time to time you will even see a man walk into a club, realize he's already hooked up with 80 percent of the women in there, and immediately focus on the lone holdouts. It's a sight to behold, one of truly intense focus and applied tunnel vision, akin to watching Derek Jeter work the room at a *Maxim* party. But as these Jersey Shore virgins begin to learn the ropes, they quickly gain a

deep understanding of the region's social mores that will ultimately be transmitted to their hometowns by word of mouth. In many ways, it's like the vast pollination of dandelions, but with more hair gel.

As quickly as the madness descends upon these sleepy coastal towns, however, it vanishes into the ether. And it is only when the dust settles and these towns are left to pick up the pieces that we can begin to analyze what has just transpired here at the Shore. Where these temporary inhabitants go in the interim is anyone's guess. No one is really sure exactly what sorts of activities Guidos and Guidettes get up to during the winter. It is widely assumed that they hibernate in the far reaches of New York and New England, where the frozen tundra obscures even the hint of a base tan. Through extensive data analysis of boardwalk shops throughout the Shore, it appears that Axe Body Spray sales historically fall approximately 58 percent between the months of November and February. That, coupled with the trail of condom wrappers and

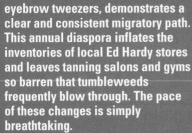

eyebrow tweezers, demonstrates a clear and consistent migratory path. This annual diaspora inflates the inventories of local Ed Hardy stores and leaves tanning salons and gyms so barren that tumbleweeds frequently blow through. The pace of these changes is simply breathtaking.

Since this summer period can represent such a whirlwind, it may be a lot to take in for someone just learning the culture. Given the unique migratory patterns of the Guido species, we thought it appropriate to introduce you, the fair reader, to the social dynamics and constructs prevalent within these tight-knit communities. Over the course of this long and winding road, we hope to introduce you to all of the fascinating facets of Guido and Guidette culture, so that you will have been armed appropriately to one day take a trip there yourself and experience the absurdity first-hand; or, if you happen to be one of the lucky ones who can actually call the Jersey Shore home, perhaps it's finally time to learn how to start fitting in. The route we travel may meander from time to time, but we hope to provide you with a comprehensive view on how best to reach your Guido or Guidette aspirations. In short, consider this book your bible.

Warm Regards,
Guido DiErio and Rick "The Happenstance" Marinara

THE SHORE WASN'T BUILT IN A DAY (IT ACTUALLY TOOK FOUR OR FIVE BECAUSE OF UNION REGULATIONS)

Historical and Economic Progress

It would be foolhardy to assume that a squadron of Guido and Guidette recruits could learn how to conduct themselves properly and truly attune their respective behaviors to the Shore without acknowledging the forebears of the Guido movement. While the word "Guido" was once only a term of derision, the name has evolved into a rallying cry, with scores of young men and women using the word as a banner of pride. Today's Guidos and Guidettes have taken the baton from the revered Guidos of the past, whose blood, sweat, and hair gel paved the way for such a beautiful confluence of cultural touchstones.

As we look back, the events of Guido history fall naturally into several distinct epochs. Each time period saw notable developments in cultural progress, so in an effort to provide as much clarity as possible, we have outlined the salient achievements of each era for your personal consumption. It was the least we could do.

The Bronzer Age

The primitive Guido culture at the Jersey Shore was far different from the technological advancement you see today (hey, sending picture mail on your cell phone of your genitals demonstrates at least an elementary understanding of communication). These prehistoric creatures were limited in terms of conversing with one another, but eventually they formed a primitive language. The first tentative attempts at contact were somewhat stilted, relying heavily on grunts, pointing, and body language. In many ways, this parallels what you will see if you happen to wander into a gym on the Shore (albeit with more pulsating veins).

The gender dynamics of this time period were distinctive as well. In those days, males dominated every aspect of cultural interaction, with the expectation that the terms they dictated would be the prevailing laws of their fledgling communities. Consequently, when a male forced himself on a woman sexually, females tended to tragically capitulate rather than be ostracized by their societies. OK, apparently not that much has changed. The only difference would be that eons ago, males tended to employ threats of mayhem by blunt trauma, whereas now, young Guidos have a variety of high-gravity alcohols to induce bad decision-making. (NOTE: Many energy drinks have come out with roofie-inspired flavors to help streamline this process.)

As societies became slightly more advanced, though, these primitive Guidos and Guidettes were soon able to fashion crude tools and items of necessity for their survival. This meant spears for hunting so they could form the basis of an incredibly protein-rich diet, as well as the historical precursors of dumbbells so muscles could be sculpted even while not on the hunt. Women too proved to be ingenious inventors, utilizing ferns and

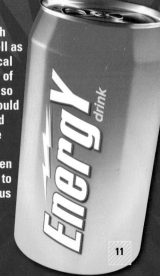

other pliable plants to form unsophisticated hair ties that they could use to create the predecessor of the poof. But the hallmark invention of this time was a smooth, flat slab of granite that was used as a makeshift tanning bed. This, coupled with the roots from certain plants and the pigments from ores in the prehistoric Shore, helped form a nice base tan that would only get more pronounced as time moved on.

From Colonies to a Modern Society (1776 to 1899)

Skipping forward to the dawn of America, Guidos at the time of the Revolutionary War were renowned for their crafty fighting skills and battlefield tactics. Their blown-out hairstyles meant that tri-cornered hats were not an option, which enabled them to more easily blend in with the woods in which they were hiding. The application of bronzer also contributed a camouflage effect that enabled their leader, Brigadier General Ronnie Del Monte, to orchestrate a series of impressive attacks that captured large swathes of territory for American colonial forces. New Jersey would be rewarded for all its bravery and heroics by receiving statehood on December 18, 1787.

Technological developments also helped the Shore make a name for itself. In an immense boost to state pride, Thomas Edison invented the incandescent lightbulb in 1879 in the sleepy town of Menlo Park. While this invention clearly has transformed the quality of life in many parts of the world, the original applications for this revolutionary method of harnessing electricity were much simpler and focused on the surrounding environs. Edison actually had a fair amount of trouble convincing utilities to invest in capital-intensive electrical grid infrastructure, since the tanning beds that were developed around that time drew massive amounts of power and plagued the Northeast with rolling blackouts. Sadly, this period of time was beset with limited electricity and uneven tans. Truly a tragedy.

The seminal moment of the century for the Jersey Shore was the completion of the boardwalk in 1890. This allowed for the linkage of community to community, with each plank representing a willingness to bridge the gaps of whatever differences might exist in these towns. The boardwalk also created a thriving marketplace for vendors to hawk their wares, creating an opportunity for entrepreneurial would-be chefs to sell their corn dogs, cotton candy, and taffy away from the ominous specter of food and beverage regulatory bodies. The boardwalk's value would only be fully realized decades later, as budding Guidos and Guidettes began to find the catacombs beneath the planks to be optimal locations for inebriated copulation.

Modern History (1900s to present)

To highlight the trials and tribulations of the Jersey Shore and the rise of its social mores, we found it made the most sense to look at a smattering of individual events and try to assess their collective significance. This timeline should help provide you with a deep understanding of the major historical events and changes of the last century, as American society as a whole surged into the modern era. In contrast, most places in the Jersey Shore started getting the Internet in 2007. Food for thought.

Timeline

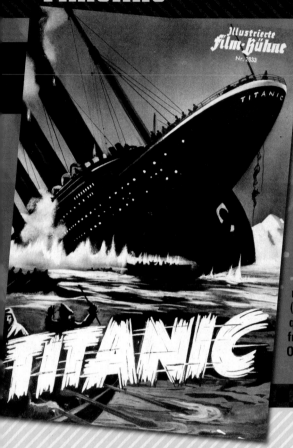

1912:

On a trip from Southampton to New York City, the RMS *Titanic* strikes an iceberg and sinks shortly thereafter. Not only will this spawn the preeminent chick flick of our time (sorry, *The Notebook*), but the phrase "that broad went down on me faster than the Titanic" (or derivations thereof) is quickly adopted in towns from Long Branch to Ocean City.

1921:

A gentleman in Point Pleasant Beach inadvertently starts the Guido Frolic when— after slipping on a banana peel while attempting to do the Charleston—his feet start moving at an incredible rate of speed. Yes, someone actually slipped on a banana peel. And you thought that only happened in cartoons.

930S:

e Great Depression is
rvasive throughout the U.S., as
s are lost and the economy
sps for life. This condition is
ghtly more acute among the
rsey seaside communities,
here a profound lack of quality
air products contributes to an
nveloping sense of misery that
vill not be shaken off for years.

1955:

Sandy Dennoloti introduces the
hair extension to the American
populace, thrilling a legion of
Guidettes who demand longer,
fuller hair. Sadly, these products
will also be abused by males in
the future, with Fabio and that
shitty band Nelson being the
major offenders.

1961:

The Bay of Pigs Invasion, the CIA's secretive attempt to
remove Fidel Castro as leader of Cuba, is splashed all
over the headlines in an embarrassing black eye for
American politics. This incident only creates a state of
mass confusion throughout the Jersey Shore, as
everyone just assumes the title of the event refers to the
quality of the women in Sandy Hook Bay.

1968:

In a glorious act of civil
disobedience, Tommie Smith
and John Carlos raise their
fists (covered in black gloves)
to the heavens after winning
medals in track and field at the
Mexico City Summer Olympics.
Not only is this communal
gesture a watershed event in
the American civil rights
landscape, but it is widely
believed that the strength and
grace expressed by those fists
will set the scene for the most
popular of all Guido dance
moves.

15

973: The Arab oil embargo and subsequent oil crisis chokes off shipments of precious fossil fuels to the Eastern seaboard of the U.S. for months, forcing the Jersey Shore to institute draconian gel-rationing laws, which makes some poor souls resort to canola oil.

1977:

The movie *Saturday Night Fever* debuts to throngs of adoring audiences, with John Travolta somehow being accepted as a realistic depiction of a sex symbol. This movie proves to be a major cultural turning point for the Jersey attitude, as well as showing how this bravado can be expressed via dance. The movie also makes the Bee Gees incredibly popular throughout America, a fact that still haunts its producers to this day.

1978:

Following his role in *Saturday Night Fever*, Travolta pairs with Olivia Newton-John in the movie adaptation of the musical *Grease*. This film touches on many current aspects of the Shore, including the phenomenon of "summer love," an enthusiasm for dousing one's hair in product, and Travolta's friends pushing him to spill the details of his sordid sex romps (a scene that is effectively recreated at every barber shop in the U.S.).

1981:

Ricky Bevilacqua is credited for making the "fist pump heard around the world." Though hailed as a groundbreaker for being the first to introduce this move to dance halls throughout the Shore, it is believed in some circles that Mr. Bevilacqua did not actually intend this trendsetting move. He actually slipped on some wayward hair product and threw a punch due to force of habit.

1983:

Consumer products conglomerate Unilever unveils its new product line of spray deodorants, Axe Body Spray. It's expected that in 2010, these miniature canisters of stank contribute to one-third of current New Jersey landfill usage, though they are known to make a handy flame-thrower in a pinch.

1986:

New Jersey's own Bon Jovi releases their definitive album *Slippery When Wet*. Ironically, the Guido movement suffers repeated backlash throughout the late 1980s due to the sudden rise in popularity of feathered hair, until the hair band movement is effectively murdered by Def Leppard (though that band was responsible for a brief spike in nine-armed music groups).

1989:

The petrochemical industry takes a massive hit in the wake of the *Exxon Valdez* spill in Alaskan waters. This shock again permeates the global gel and hair markets, spurring several congressmen in New Jersey to lobby for additional research and development funds to be dedicated to the advancement of fibrous follicle technologies. The bill sputters in committee.

The fall of the Berlin Wall starts to dismantle the Iron Curtain of Communism in Eastern Europe, as former Soviet satellites push for their independence and demonstrate a severe desire to plug into the rest of the world. This allows a variety of Eurotrash DJs (who formerly would have been forced into low-stress state employment) to now spin a vast assortment of unimaginative house music that will eventually become a staple of every club on the Shore.

1990:

The fist pump begins to gain acceptance in mainstream society after Arsenio Hall introduces it on his show after interviewing Earvin "Magic" Johnson. As an aside, it's still amazing that the most famously contracted sexually transmitted disease on earth is held by a man named MAGIC JOHNSON. You can't make this stuff up.

1991:

Armani spins off the brand Armani Exchange in an effort to extend its appeal to the general populace beyond its original high-end clientele. In no time at all, this brand becomes a staple of every Guido wardrobe. You'd have to be a fool to pass up the opportunity to spend $140 on a black t-shirt with no writing on it.

1992:

An affair featuring Joey Buttafuoco (a Guido elder statesman who lives with his wife in Long Island) and his then-underage turboskank, Amy Fisher, becomes national news after the young Fisher shoots Buttafuoco's wife in the face. Ms. Fisher is sentenced to seven years in jail for this incident (though she later makes decent money providing hunting tips to Dick Cheney).

1993:

Walker, Texas Ranger premieres on CBS. OK, this doesn't really have anything to do with the Guido movement, but can we all just agree that Chuck Norris rocks fucking hard? He could totally have a sick blowout too, if he'd just ditch the cowboy hat.

1994: Crayola makes some stark revisions to its classic sixty-four-color box. Tangerine is changed to "Guido Tan Orange," lending further legitimacy to the evolving Guido culture, as well as finally providing society at large with a name for this curious tint.

1996: After watching one of the 4,239 times *Dances with Wolves* airs on TBS, Wildwood miscreant Pauly Pepitone decides to get an ornate tribal tattoo crafted around his biceps. Seriously, what an asshole.

2000:

Partying with her gal pals for her twenty-third birthday, Angela Dellabonte debuts a lower-back tattoo at the Bamboo Bar in Seaside Heights that is estimated to be over four feet in total area. This "mother of all tramp stamps" is the current world record holder for "Most Overt Display of Inevitable Sexual Promiscuity," and is widely considered to have been the impetus for copycat artwork that will define the decade.

2002:

Following years of clinical testing and trial and error in laboratories throughout America, the first successful calf implant takes place in Margate, New Jersey. This landmark surgery allows men throughout the region to be just as insecure about their looks as their female counterparts, which is saying something.

2004:

The infamous Hot Tub Outbreak of 2004 claims the genitals of over 220 Guidos and Guidettes, leaving a trail of itching, swelling, and incredibly awkward phone calls and text messages to former one-night stands.

2007:

Inspired by Navy SEALs, the Perfect Pushup comes onto the market. This product is universally hailed by Guidos as a great way to work on your upper body at all times, while simultaneously flushing your money down the toilet.

2008:

The world is rocked by a catastrophic global financial crisis which threatens the very basis of capitalism and free trade that underpins the buying and selling of goods and services. Through the selling of complex financial instruments like credit default swaps and collateralized debt obligations, many financial institutions take risky bets and become massively overleveraged, causing the loss of trillions of dollars in equity in stock exchanges worldwide. In other news, at least twelve people throughout the Jersey Shore open checking accounts during the fiscal year.

2009 TO PRESENT DAY:

Two Words:
Jersey Shore

Gross Domestic Product (GDP) Components of the Jersey Shore

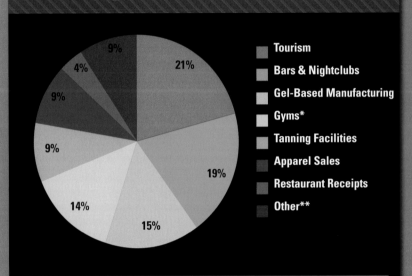

- Tourism — 21%
- Bars & Nightclubs — 19%
- Gel-Based Manufacturing — 15%
- Gyms* — 14%
- Tanning Facilities — 9%
- Apparel Sales — 9%
- Restaurant Receipts — 4%
- Other** — 9%

*Includes both gym facilities and personal-training revenues; approximately 91% of Jersey Shore males identify themselves as "personal trainer."
**"Other" encompasses receipts from ferris wheel rides, boardwalk plank construction, carnival game revenues, morning-after pill sales, condom sales, and R&D dedicated to spur herpes research.

As you're packing your bags for an incredible time at the Shore, regardless of the length of your stay, you may start to wonder about how the economy of the region works. Or you may not. As the possessor of an education that could charitably be referred to as "rudimentary," there's a good chance you've overlooked things like "how to sustain one's self financially." It should be comforting to know, however, that just like your hometown, the Shore is subject to the simple economic tenets of supply and demand. It hasn't always been this way, though, as the region's economy was primarily based on the bartering of hoop earrings and bronzer until the mid-twentieth century. This is similar in many ways to the fact that you could get a

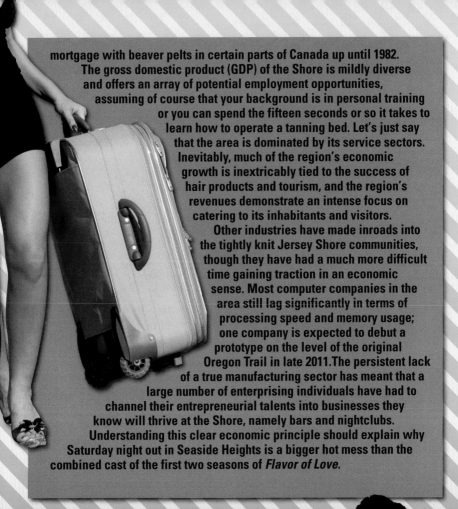

mortgage with beaver pelts in certain parts of Canada up until 1982. The gross domestic product (GDP) of the Shore is mildly diverse and offers an array of potential employment opportunities, assuming of course that your background is in personal training or you can spend the fifteen seconds or so it takes to learn how to operate a tanning bed. Let's just say that the area is dominated by its service sectors. Inevitably, much of the region's economic growth is inextricably tied to the success of hair products and tourism, and the region's revenues demonstrate an intense focus on catering to its inhabitants and visitors.

Other industries have made inroads into the tightly knit Jersey Shore communities, though they have had a much more difficult time gaining traction in an economic sense. Most computer companies in the area still lag significantly in terms of processing speed and memory usage; one company is expected to debut a prototype on the level of the original Oregon Trail in late 2011.The persistent lack of a true manufacturing sector has meant that a large number of enterprising individuals have had to channel their entrepreneurial talents into businesses they know will thrive at the Shore, namely bars and nightclubs. Understanding this clear economic principle should explain why Saturday night out in Seaside Heights is a bigger hot mess than the combined cast of the first two seasons of *Flavor of Love*.

Cultural Events

Uh ... Andrew Dice Clay did a reunion tour here in '97 and ... uh ... seriously, no one has actually ever inquired about these things. I mean, a library burned down twenty miles outside of Ocean City and was replaced with a mixed-use facility that incorporated a tanning salon with a protein synthesis factory. Perhaps that will help you understand the region's priorities a little better. But some of the pamphlets at the free clinic have gotten pretty fancy though, eh? Eat your heart out *The Atlantic*.

Conclusion

Having a deep understanding of the defining moments that have left indelible marks on each of the Shore's communities is an important step in gaining the experience you need to truly maximize your opportunities as a Guido. After all, those who don't learn from history are doomed to repeat it. **(NOTE: That is especially true of your late-night dalliances with the opposite sex.)** Each of these events managed to build like a crescendo, and the whole is clearly more than the sum of its parts. These trendsetters and innovators managed to shape the Shore in a particularly unique way, eventually manifesting itself in the Sodom and Gomorrah you can see in the present day (which makes New Orleans during Mardi Gras look like a nunnery convention). As you press on, learning how to shape every aspect of your body and personality to total Guidofication, at least remember to recognize the efforts of all those who came before you. Pouring out some of your Red Bull and vodka would be a nice gesture.

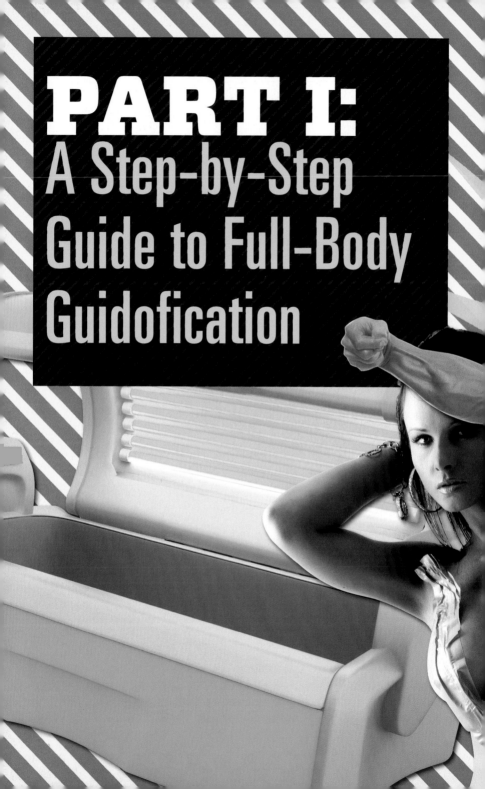

PART I:
A Step-by-Step Guide to Full-Body Guidofication

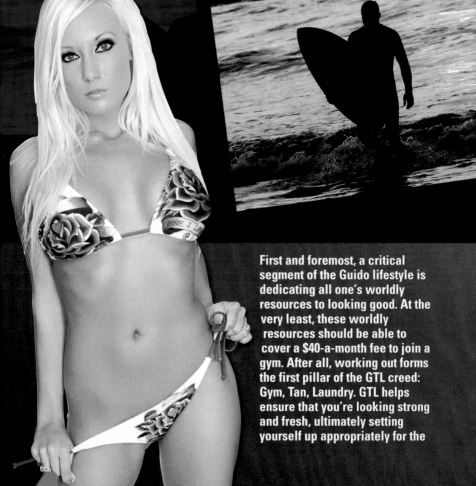

THE ABCs (ABS, BICEPS, CHEST) . . . OR, A GUIDO'S GUIDE TO THE GYM

First and foremost, a critical segment of the Guido lifestyle is dedicating all one's worldly resources to looking good. At the very least, these worldly resources should be able to cover a $40-a-month fee to join a gym. After all, working out forms the first pillar of the GTL creed: Gym, Tan, Laundry. GTL helps ensure that you're looking strong and fresh, ultimately setting yourself up appropriately for the complicated mating ritual that will undoubtedly take place during your time at the Shore. However, it's not as easy as just stepping into your local 24-Hour Fitness, wading through the stench, and finding the one functioning machine; there's a lot more that goes into honing a body. The process of selecting a gym is critical, as is deciding what exercises to focus on, choosing what to wear, and picking the appropriate post-gym routines.

Moreover, it's important to remember that in order to see results that will allow your veins to bulge to dizzying heights and to create a persona that will undoubtedly frighten small children, hitting the gym daily is absolutely critical to your success. Your goal should not be just to show up to work out, but to actually get some time in and hit it hard. They don't give awards for participation at the Jersey Shore. If you don't like it, stick to youth soccer and enjoy the orange slices and Capri Sun.

That means for the Guidos, we're talking about at least an hour and a half, maybe two, hours of high-quality meatheadedness. For the Guidettes, it's approximately the same (though let's be honest, all women do at the gym is talk on the phone while on an elliptical machine). Anything shorter than that, and you may as well be walking around with a fanny pack, water wings, and flip-flops, because you'll just be a tourist. For the amount of time you could fritter away millions of brain cells watching a Rob Schneider movie, you could actually be focusing on building a body that will make you the envy of everyone else at the gym, and perhaps even gawked at and pointed to on the beach. It also goes without saying that you're hitting the gym every day of the week and twice on Sundays.

Choosing a Gym

The right gym should be so chock-full of testosterone that even Major League Baseball would admit it's "a bit much." You are shooting for an atmosphere akin to the two or three minutes before an MMA fight starts, when there is always the palpable sense that you may actually witness someone get pummeled into oblivion. (NOTE: This includes both the fighters and the crowd.) If the gym also has that highly unsettling sound that plays every time the

Joker appears in *The Dark Knight*, that's a bonus. The good thing about having more pent-up rage than every episode of HBO's *Oz* is that it will foster good-natured competition and help you push yourself. Or, it will lead to the first-ever grand jury convocation about second-degree murder by medicine ball. Really, there's no middle ground.

A true Guidette should be focused on finding a gym that makes her feel like she's been dropped onto the set of *Gorillas in the Mist*, except in this case, the mist would be provided by the spray from opening a can of Red Bull. This offers her the opportunity to focus not only on hitting the cardio hard, but also on finding potential steroid-fueled Guido mates who can woo her by offering all the appurtenances of a luxurious lower-class lifestyle in a split-level in Parnassus. As with the guys, the good-natured competition between women should lead to fantastic results, as long as no hairspray is applied prior to your gym session (given that Jersey girls notoriously forget to ash their cigarettes while using recumbent bikes).

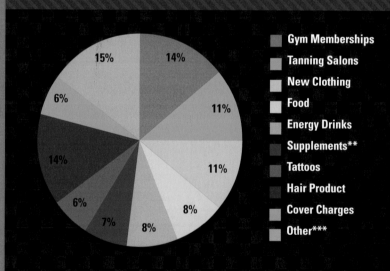

Applications for Disposable Income Among Guidos & Guidettes (2010)*

- Gym Memberships
- Tanning Salons
- New Clothing
- Food
- Energy Drinks
- Supplements**
- Tattoos
- Hair Product
- Cover Charges
- Other***

14% 11% 11% 8% 8% 7% 6% 14% 6% 15%

*If this seems grossly oversimplified, just remember that a significant percentage of this population derives their income from lotto scratcher tickets.
**Includes both legal and illegal.
***"Other" encompasses a variety of different items not included above, including educational materials, university tuition, travel abroad, books, magazines that are not explicitly about MMA, and donations to NPR.

Beyond the atmosphere, there are a myriad of other items to consider when selecting a facility. You should focus on a place that's relatively new and was not forced to buy a selection of used pig-iron weights from a Soviet yard sale. Decent ventilation is important as well. We're not saying it needs to be like a wind tunnel in there, but some of our most impure odors have a way of sticking around in places they're not wanted. Some gyms you'll visit smell like a devilish concoction of a well-used gas station bathroom on a major trucking route and a funeral parlor at the height of summer in Arizona. Finding a place that offers a substantial cross-section of attractive potential mates is also a critical step in the selection process, especially since you have the opportunity to view each option through the (occasionally) embarrassing prism of limited clothing.

Other nontraditional factors that go into choosing a gym may focus on creature comforts and amenities, if you're into that sort of thing. Some places offer juice bars, which, although they can get somewhat pricey, function essentially like singles bars. It's like being magically whisked away to one of the hot new clubs at the Shore, only with less alcohol, less fist-pumping, and more visible tramp stamps (OK, the last point is arguable). Other folks look for a place with a Jacuzzi, though it is recommended you think long and hard about how crucial that hot tub is. (NOTE: Let's just say that the New Jersey-borne herpes and syphilis strains have developed a resistance to boiling water and are plotting a major offensive on the Atlantic seaboard in 2017.)

The point is, whether you are looking for a basic gym that will offer you just the latest and greatest in equipment or want to go for all the bells and whistles, you'll be making a trade-off. Nice gyms cost money. Since Goldman Sachs and J.P. Morgan still tend to focus on hiring employees with "applied intelligence," "social skills," and "the good sense not to attempt to settle every potential disagreement with some type of physical violence," it may be difficult for you to afford the kind of establishment used by Manhattan's upper crust. If you apply this handy metric to allocate your spending, you will probably get a good sense of what is in your price range.

Dressing the Part

A great deal of the gym experience is wrapped up in what you're wearing, or, in some cases, not wearing. Whoever said "clothes make the man" clearly didn't have big guns. The best scenario for a Guido would actually be to find a gym that would let you work out sans shirt, but the only facilities that will generally show you any leeway on that are at outdoor beaches or detention centers. The first option usually provides you with weights covered in seagull crap, and the second . . .

well . . . probably no need to explore that in greater detail. Given that these byzantine restrictions remain in place, you should go for the next best option: the shirt with no sleeves.

Shirts without sleeves are perfect for the gym, as they allow you ample time to stare intently at the muscles you're developing, as well as to glance over at the new Chinese symbol (that loosely translates to "unimaginative douchebag" in English) emblazoned on your left biceps. Rocking the "allergic to sleeves" look is also very practical for the actual lifting process, as you won't be encumbered by all those micrograms of sleeve weight the t-shirt companies have been foisting upon you for years. The best option in this case is to go with a tank top, though you may prefer the ripped-sleeve look since it will make you look like the owner of a dojo. If you have no other option but to wear a t-shirt, at least opt for one with a phrase on it that is meant to intimidate male gym-goers. "Tapout" will make them think some sort of chokehold is immediately forthcoming, and "Affliction" will make them think you are the possessor of one or more deep-seated psychological problems. Or, try a phrase that lewdly informs female gym-goers what you would like to do with them (there is a dizzying array of genital-based t-shirt humor at your disposal). Both track pants and shorts are acceptable options, though clearly jean shorts are precluded from this discussion.

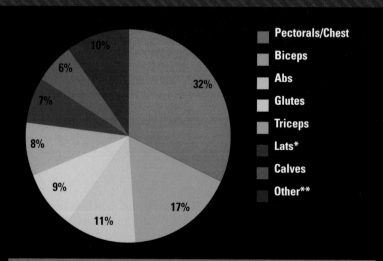

Muscles that Contribute Heavily to Getting Laid (2010)

- Pectorals/Chest — 32%
- Biceps — 17%
- Abs — 11%
- Glutes — 9%
- Triceps — 8%
- Lats* — 7%
- Calves — 6%
- Other** — 10%

*Yes. Some people out there actually dig lats.
**"Other" encompasses muscles like delts, forearms, quadriceps, and a variety of smaller fibers that control movement in the wrists and ankles.

Weightlifting Philosophy

There are a plethora of words to describe the benefits of going to a gym: getting cut, ripped, swole, huge, massive, steroidal, etc. The only thing bigger than the guys who do the lifting is the volume of terms used to describe the activity in the first place. Beyond the simple matter of denoting your slow metamorphosis into half-man, half-gorilla, a Guido's focus should be to work on one thing and one thing only: your glamour muscles. These also go by the moniker "beach muscles" for the uninitiated. Essentially, these are the types of body parts that will look good in the metric gallon of Crisco you regularly use to oil yourself up. Despite the obvious physical benefits of trying to form a well-rounded physical being, you shouldn't worry about building muscles that aren't immediately visible when you are unclothed, because when was the last time you heard of trapezius muscles getting you laid?

Your workout should focus on three major areas (a.k.a. your ABCs): abs, biceps, and chest. From a fitness perspective, your arms are probably going to be the first thing a girl sees, for better or for worse. If you have the muscle tone of Jared pre-Subway, you can rest assured that the only dates you'll have lined up are with Rosy Palm and her five friends. Packing two guns is a much more attractive look. You should be trying to cultivate a look in which wearing your favorite Ed Hardy shirts may actually cut off circulation in your arms for extended periods of time. Developing muscle tone in your chest is a must as well, even if it may mean you have to change certain habits, like walking through doors.

As for your abs, you basically want to have the whole Michael Phelps thing going on, without the penchant for jailbait and bongrips. Your goal shouldn't just be to have a six-pack, but for each segment of your six-pack to have a six-pack. That's right. A thirty-six-pack. Once you start thinking exponentially, you will really start to see results (though admittedly, you may need to brush up on seventh-grade math). And just think, if each part of your thirty-six-pack had a six-pack . . . the mind boggles.

It's not enough to actually get in a workout that breaks down muscles in order to build them up stronger. That's how a novice lifts. A truly advanced Guido not only will be able to maintain this sort of basic workout regimen, but will also branch out into ridiculous displays of strength and agility in order to assert his rightful place in the pecking order of his chosen establishment. These activities may include doing spinning kicks on a heavy bag or performing exercises that take up large swathes of territory. But unquestionably, the best way to "peacock" at one of these gyms is to commit yourself to a philosophy as old as time itself: lifting way more than your body can possibly handle.

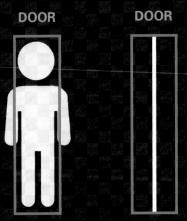

DOOR   **DOOR**

The fellow on the left is clearly too developed in his shoulders to walk through the door he encounters correctly; the gentleman on the right (who is shown in profile view) can enter the door by side-stepping into the door.

Arms

There are a lot of different exercises that can help out those arms, bro. Barbell curls, triceps dips and extensions, preacher curls—there's no shortage. There are even things you can do around the house to strengthen your arms, like move spare tire rims that are in your foyer for some reason, or quietly pick up passed-out visitors who have out-stayed their welcome to take them to locations more hospitable than your living room. The point is, you always have to be thinking when it comes to working out, and you can find some quick and dirty ways to get your lift on, chief. It should be noted that doing twelve-ounce curls of Heineken's is not recommended because—although consistent repetitions will help you develop some modicum of tone—the weight is still too small and you will be doing nothing to construct the shrine you desire on your midsection. It's recommended that you find six to eight arm workouts that you like and vary them often so your body doesn't get time to adapt, much as your skin will tend to return to its disgusting pale color instead of the desired nuclear tangerine shade if not exposed to a barrage of gamma rays at your tanning salon.

One specific workout that not only offers tangible real-world applications, but also is fun to do and will get your heart moving, is the fist pump workout. In this case, you simply grab a weight that will provide some degree of resistance and start dancing away as if your favorite DJ has just taken over the turntables. Once you begin your fist-pumping motion, you will really start to feel the burn and, if you're doing the exercise correctly, you will probably start to feel ligaments tearing in your elbow, as well as early warning signs of a first-degree shoulder separation. It's also important to note that you should perform this exercise using both arms

as the fist-pumping fulcrum; otherwise, you will completely overdevelop one arm and look like one of those freakish arm-wrestling champions with the thin mustaches from Eastern Europe. Not an attractive look. Additional side effects from overdeveloping one arm include swimming in circles and potentially catastrophic episodes of masturbation. A benefit to using both arms (beyond a well-developed physique) is that you will be one of the few members of the Jersey Shore community who can fist-pump ambidextrously, which is like being a switch-hitter for the Yankees in Seaside.

For the Guidettes, your focus should really be on limiting the amount of weight you lift on your biceps and triceps, focusing instead on maximum repetitions. This will help tone the body and really develop the arms you've been looking for. It's not even about ending up with Michelle Obama arms, it's more of a question of trying not to have giant mounds of salt water taffy where your triceps should be. That's something you have to nip in the bud when you're young, because once you hit your thirties and are inhaling ricotta cheese like it's your job, those flabby triceps are going to make you look like a flying squirrel. It's bad enough as it is, but if and when a stiff wind comes up, you're liable to end up in Long Island. Think about it.

Shoulders

In addition to having a well-developed set of pythons and a chest that makes you look like an extra from *300*, working on your shoulders will provide a wonderful complement to the rest of your body. This area is also more important than you may realize in your day-to-day life. Lifting up the lid at the tanning salon? Reaching for the pesto sauce you put on the top shelf? Carrying your girlfriend home from the club because she drank so much she'd make Lindsay Lohan blush? All of these instances require crucial slow-twitch muscles in your shoulders that you can hone through careful cultivation. Your first introduction to the wonderful world of shoulder exercises: the shoulder shrug.

The shoulder shrug is simplicity itself. Pick up weight, lower shoulders, lift up shoulders. The only thing you're going to find that's easier than that is a bachelorette party in Seaside Heights. Before selecting how much weight to lift, it is recommended you use at least a pound of chalk on your hands or use lifting gloves that require six or seven Velcro straps, and perhaps even a zipper or two. This isn't about ensuring a proper grip, though; this is merely a method by which you can capture the gaze of other patrons before totally shredding the shit out of your shoulders. Score.

In selecting weight, the classic rule you should follow is to pick a weight you could do comfortably, multiply by two, and then add forty.

(NOTE: This is the type of incredibly scientific formula that led to Hollywood green-lighting the movie *Paul Blart: Mall Cop*.) You will know you're doing it correctly if it feels like your shoulders are going to pop out of their sockets. Don't worry, that's just the adrenaline. After selecting a pair of weights, just grip tight, drop down, and lift back up. Your focus should be less on the weights you're holding and more on making a series of guttural grunts and off-putting sounds that will further attract attention to yourself and let everyone bask in your awesomeness. Life is good.

You can also perform other exercises that will key on these muscles, like lat pull-downs or military-style presses. The latter is especially recommended because it makes you sound like a real bad-ass. All things considered, the other major benefit to both working out your shoulders and doing such a diverse array of exercises to achieve your results is that you will affect other ancillary muscles as well. Performing these exercises properly will make it difficult for many admirers to tell where your neck stops and where your shoulders begin. This "Frankenstein Theory" is a happy by-product of all your hard work, and should pay off as long as the villagers don't come to your time-share with torches and pitchforks. (NOTE: Worst-case scenario.)

Chest

The chest is another important area for the guys to put serious time into developing. The bench press has always been the true bellwether of a gentleman's fitness and sexual prowess, so great heed should be paid to developing your pectoral area. Push-ups are obviously a great start, and you can bang those out right in front of the TV so as not to interfere with your *Price Is Right* reruns, FreeCreditReport.com commercials, and *Judge Joe Brown*. But the real value is in the gym itself, where you'll find a dizzying array of free weights, machines, and 300-pound guys who don't appear to have any mailing address other than the corner of the gym with the bench press. It's tragically beautiful, really. Once there, you can do all sorts of variations on the bench press—regular, inclined, declined—the world is your oyster. (NOTE: Declined bench presses should be done only by professionals, as your top-heavy status will leave you highly susceptible to doing backward somersaults into other patrons in an ass-over-teakettle fashion.)

The regular bench press is still the gold standard of the gym, though. This is where you'll have to put in your time if you really want to start seeing results. In a similar vein to other exercises, a standard strategy to start with on the bench press is to lift more than you can realistically hope to attain. This is how you break down and build muscle, as well as test the theoretical limits of the COBRA health care you have in place since you lost your job at the taffy parlor. (NOTE: Sadly, taffy is a discretionary expenditure that historically fares poorly in times of economic duress; truly, taffy sales are one of the most reliable economic indicators.)

In approaching the bench, you should strive to grab the largest plates possible and make a fairly audible dog-and-pony show about the amount you are about to lift. Having spotters who will not only provide lifting support but also perform the crucial role of homoerotically cheering you on is imperative, as one should never lift alone. This is not due to any safety considerations, however; the main reason you want to lift with other dudes is to ensure that you will constantly be making more noise than the four a.m. garbage collection and

generally make a solid spectacle of yourselves.

As you're actually lifting the weight, you should focus on smooth, fluid motions, a far cry from the herky-jerky movements you demonstrate on the dance floor. Leveraging your spotter on each side, you should aim for only one or two repetitions and maximize the weight you lift, in keeping with the principle that for every repetition you make, you should spend an additional fifteen minutes talking about it. You should take great care as you lift the bar up and down, making sure to keep this potentially deadly weapon a safe distance away from your throat. There's no worse come-on at the bars than trying to say something borderline offensive to a hottie but realizing she can't hear you because your crushed larynx makes you sound like one of those people from the anti-tobacco ads who talk through a voicebox.

As for the Guidettes, uh . . . well . . . uh . . . the assumption is you have implants. You have implants? We thought you had implants. So you've got the implants. OK, good, so we're all in agreement. Let's just move on.

Abs

The core of your body is essential to take care of for many reasons. It is the source of much of your power, and if you take care of it, it will take care of you. Ask any dude with lower back pain in his mid-forties if he should have gone to that core class during his lunch breaks when he was younger, and he will probably give you the finger (albeit with considerable pain). Beyond the fact that so much of your happiness and well-being springs from this critical body part, it is also vitally important to demonstrate your progress in abs development by repeatedly lifting your shirt, pointing at your abs, and smiling with the vacant air of triumph you demonstrated when you got your University of Phoenix diploma in the mail.

There is really no shortage of ways to work out your midsection, though the most easily identifiable exercises are sit-ups and basic crunches. While some folks hammer out five or six hundred sit-ups a day, all this effort might be for naught if (a) your approach is flawed or (b) you're just flat-out doing it wrong. You should focus intently on flexing your stomach muscles during each repetition, as that's how you're going to start seeing that six-pack you crave. Your goal should be a stomach so hard you can grate cheese on it (which may come in handy should you find yourself with a block of Parmesan and none of the requisite tools).

Beyond just straight crunches, you should also make sure to incorporate exercises that will build your oblique muscles. Not doing this would be like souping up the engine of your car but still rolling around on stock hubcaps: an unforgivable sin. Doing side crunches or utilizing a stability ball will help you target these occasionally hard-to-reach areas. If you can get past the unfortunate social stigma attached to using these stability balls (which could potentially make you look like one of those goateed douchebags who work at a hip Web 2.0 company),

you will find that it has an amazing ability to make you use all the muscles in your midsection in order to keep yourself from falling over.

The good thing about these exercises is that they are also valuable to each gender, as Guidettes are going to want to adopt a similar mantra in developing their cores. This may not manifest itself in a traditional six-pack, but all the same, it will focus on the process of lean-muscle building. This is a good thing, as women working too hard at developing their abs and making their muscles bulge could begin to give off a distinctly East German vibe. That's all well and good, though the development of pencil-thin mustaches will undoubtedly be a deal-breaker in the romantic department. The Adam's apple can also be a tad unsightly.

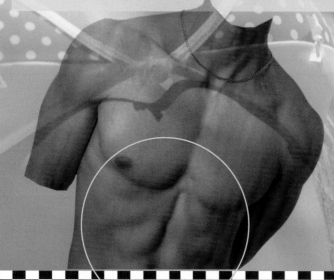

Legs

Developing your legs is probably lower on the totem pole than building up the more prominent arm muscles that ladies will flock to immediately. In effect, these muscles function very much like the offensive linemen of your body. You'll rarely focus on them, but occasionally when something goes wrong, they'll be blamed (e.g., a girl thinking you have the calf development of Dakota Fanning). So sure, they are probably the area you should spend the least amount of time on, and certainly would fall behind the body's other regions in terms of weightlifting priority, but it doesn't mean they should be avoided like that girl Vanessa you met outside the free clinic.

While working your legs can be quite superfluous, the quad press is fantastic because it makes it very easy to look like the most important asshole in the gym. The great thing about the quad press is that you will typically find it available to you in several forms, including one option where you sit down and essentially extend your legs. It's not rocket science, and shouldn't be treated as such. Most often, these will be found as one of those machines where you can move the pin to your desired weight and then go to town like Bill Clinton at a Bennigan's waitress convention. The best suggestion in this case is to stick your pin in the heaviest weight (ironically, the opposite of what you should be doing while out at the clubs), then grunt your way to one rep. If you can do two, hey, go be a hero. Regardless, make sure you leave the pin at the weight you've just completed in an effort to dazzle future users of said equipment.

The other major form of the quad press is a sled-type apparatus where you lie back at an angle. The benefits of this exercise should be clearly visible. Not only do you get to load up each side with massive plates of weight (thus visible to the rest of the gym), but in order to complete your one rep safely, you should have a spotter ON EACH SIDE.

Clearly, you are the master of your domain if you require multiple lifting lieutenants. Additionally, working on your calves and hamstrings provides great value if you don't want to constantly tear muscles as a wayward by-product of your most recent steroid cycle.

For the Guidettes, having a shapely pair of legs is obviously of great value in your quest for the Guido of your dreams. As with most exercises geared toward the fairer sex, you should intend to tone as opposed to building muscle. Sure, having a pair of quads that can crush beer cans makes for an awesome party trick, but most men will be frightened of potential mid-coitus accidents involving their genitals if your thighs can easily be mistaken for tree trunks. Light calf work and hamstring stretches will assist you in your goal of having legs like one of the models from *Deal or No Deal*, except that you won't be participating in the most ridiculous game show foisted on the American people since *Tic-Tac-Dough*.

Cardio

Hey, Guidos, this section isn't really for you. Sure, you can run on the treadmill or get some sweat going on an exercise bike, but under no circumstances should you ever find yourself within the immediate vicinity of an elliptical machine. If you absolutely must do some cardio, we recommend that you focus on other activities that will serve to draw attention to yourself, such as finding a heavy bag originally meant for boxing training and practicing roundhouse kicks until you keel over. Just because you're not a master in Brazilian Jujitsu or Krav Maga doesn't mean that the rest of the gym need not live in constant fear of your fury.

Guidettes, there are many different exercises at your disposal that are essential building blocks toward your cardiovascular health. Between the StairMaster, treadmill, varieties of exercise bikes, and elliptical machines, you always can find something that will meld with your personal philosophy of getting fit. If you are going to use the StairMaster, make sure you use the one that is a fixed stepper as opposed to the version where the stairs are on some sort of conveyor system. A hungover Guidette could easily fall off the latter type of machine and cause herself grave injury. The transition from a hot mess to a hot, sweaty, injured mess is rarely graceful.

Elliptical machines remain the core exercise method for women, which makes sense given that no human being has ever gone

inside a gym that did not have at least a thirty-five-minute wait for a Precor machine. As for the amount of time you should spend on this segment of your workout, you probably want to crank up the intensity and attempt to hammer out eighty or ninety minutes. While this may seem unnecessarily intense, remember that you will inevitably drink yourself into a stupor during the course of the evening, so your main takeaway is to try to maintain caloric neutrality. You may notice that some gyms place a limit on the amount of time you can use the machines, but these rules are traditionally enforced by a staff that can, at best, charitably be referred to as "unmotivated." Don't expect any problems on that front. And to reiterate, if you see a man working out on one of these machines, please punch him solidly in the testes and point him toward the weight room.

If there's anything that's guaranteed to expose you as a gym rookie, it's the failure to maximize your workout by taking in copious amounts of protein shortly afterward. This should become as much a staple of your routine as grunting, making provocative suggestions to female patrons, and playing grab-ass with your lifting partners. There are several ways to go about ingesting the volumes of protein that will help you begin the recovery process. The most common is taking protein powders that you can purchase from Costco or the gym itself and mixing these substances into a shake with water or milk. That way, you can be the guy who always walks around with a protein shaker and is totally not a weirdo. To offset the protein, you can also walk around with a giant five-gallon jug of water to ensure proper hydration, not to mention a need to pee so frequently that you will inevitably appear in an ad for Flomax. Drinking ready-made protein shakes by EAS or Muscle Milk is also a fun and incredibly expensive method to address this concern, one that will get you universally accepted by other gym rats everywhere.

Preparing easy high-protein meals like chicken breast or ground turkey upon returning to your time-share is also a quick and dirty way to fuel your body and prepare for your next workout. You can do so either by cooking in a pan or by utilizing a George Foreman Grill, if you're one of the six people who have purchased a George Foreman Grill in the last four years. Additionally, eating meals composed exclusively of meat products will make it clear to your housemates that you have accepted your true calling as hunter-gatherer, and will help them accept the possibility that you may be clad in loincloths for the foreseeable future.

Potential "Supplements"

Against the advice of our crack legal team, we also wanted to point out that there are some—ahem—methods of hastening the process of muscle development that may or may not be legal in this country and may or may not need to be smuggled in from Mexico or certain Central American republics. For instance, you may start to wonder whether the dude benching the five hundred pounds with the zit on his shoulder the size of a cherry tomato has any sort of chemical assistance. The short answer is, yes, he probably does. Whether or not that is a road you travel down is a deep philosophical question with no definitive answer, much like "boxers or briefs?" or "should you have that twelfth Jägerbomb?" That's simply an ethical dilemma you will have to come to terms with on your own.

Should you go down the path of incorporating HGH or anabolic steroid cycles into your dietary and physical routines, you will begin to notice a variety of changes in your body that enable you to produce consistent, high-quality workout routines. As you build your lean muscle mass, you will also acquire the ability to train longer and harder as your recovery period gets shorter and shorter. The flip side to these positives is that you may undergo a metamorphosis that was not originally envisioned. A Guido may notice his testicles shrinking to microscopic levels, which may prove awkward in the midst of sexual relations; a man who cannot locate his ball sac is generally ripe for ridicule. Men may also notice an increased incidence of breast development, also known as Professional Golfer

Syndrome. Support groups to help men that have grown their own set of flapjacks have popped up throughout the tri-state area.

The other major side effect to utilizing these products is the very realistic possibility of developing "roid rage" tendencies. Users will inevitably be beset with feelings of paranoia, delusional fantasies, and irritability. Those who already have hair-triggers and overreact will find themselves going off the deep end time and time again. It is estimated that at least two in three fights throughout the clubs that dot the Jersey Shore boardwalk are at least passively connected to roid rage. Frankly, the whole roid rage phenomenon is understandable. Wouldn't you be pissed off if your balls suddenly became the size of BB gun pellets?

If you have difficulties procuring these illegal muscle-building supplements, you can always go to your local GNC and get a variety of different substances that not only are designed to help you shed weight in your wallet, but one in ten times may even work! If you are looking to trim inches off your waistline and constantly feel like your heart is about to burst out of your chest cavity, you can opt for items like Hydroxycut or Ripped Fuel. If you are looking to build muscle, you can get your hands on some andro or some creatine. If these still aren't getting you what you need, you can always swing by the local gas station and pick up some horny goat weed, which will provide a consistent metabolic boost while also giving you the sex drive of Charlie Sheen on a three-day coke binge.

45

Conclusion

Clearly, using the gym is a central tenet of Guido philosophy, and its importance to this unique culture cannot be overstated. For Guidos, determining a routine that will let you maximize your testosterone outlay and become a hulking mass of muscles, sinews, and veins will help you establish your position among other male members of the species. For Guidettes, not only will going to the gym help you slim down, tone up, and look more like Jessica Alba than Jessica Tandy, but there is also a decent chance you will meet the juicehead of your dreams at your local gymnasium. Following these simple workout routines and incorporating them into your daily life will help you slowly ~~devolve~~ evolve into the ~~Neanderthal~~ person you would like to be.

WHEN IN DOUBT, ADD MEAT SAUCE . . . OR, CRAFTING THE OPTIMAL GUIDO DIET

The dietary options available to Guidos and Guidettes are numerous, with delicious concoctions seemingly available at any hour of the day. While Italian food is similar to Mexican cuisine in some regards (e.g., dramatic overreliance on a few simple ingredients), a good chef will be able to make an imprint on any meal he or she touches. The presence of so many intriguing spices also allows the cook to perform the role of an artisan, carefully crafting each recipe to exactly reflect the delicate balance between sweet, salty, savory, and garlic (which is also its own food group). It is vital for any true Guido or Guidette to be able to put together some simple items in the kitchen, as that is an area in which you will be judged by potential mates.

Some health nuts may not be too keen on diving head-first into meals that prominently feature starches and saturated fats. With this distinct abundance of carbohydrates, the Guido and Guidette diet is enough to make Dr. Atkins roll over in his grave. (NOTE: Their eating habits would be a bigger nightmare for him than a loaf of Wonder Bread.) All things considered, though, the diet you can assemble should provide you with a diversity of rich meal options that won't leave you heavily dependent on instant ramen or Easy Mac 'n' Cheese. As soon as you figure out how best to prepare a variety of staples, you will be able to form the building blocks of your diet and craft the essential meals that will make you well known throughout the Shore.

Food Preparation

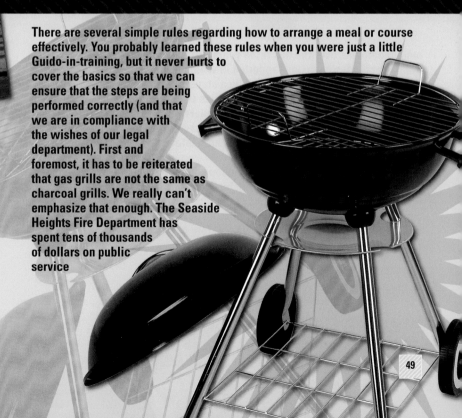

There are several simple rules regarding how to arrange a meal or course effectively. You probably learned these rules when you were just a little Guido-in-training, but it never hurts to cover the basics so that we can ensure that the steps are being performed correctly (and that we are in compliance with the wishes of our legal department). First and foremost, it has to be reiterated that gas grills are not the same as charcoal grills. We really can't emphasize that enough. The Seaside Heights Fire Department has spent tens of thousands of dollars on public service

announcements over the last three years, yet these incidents persist. Similar episodes have been reported in which Guidos have attempted to light electric ranges. Please, don't be a statistic.

The ability to chop and slice vegetables correctly is invaluable, as this simple skill ends up being a vital part of nearly every recipe you'll have to put together. Care in this regard also helps create smaller portions of food so that Guidos and Guidettes avoid choking fatalities. (NOTE: Red bell peppers and LEGOS are the primary contributors to Guido windpipe-related injuries.) You should try and chop vegetables down so they will add nice color and texture to a meal, but be careful not to be overzealous in these efforts. Going overboard may actually create a fine powder, which can be inhaled if the wind patterns are not in your favor. Great care should also be taken to be meticulous in your safety precautions. You're there to cut parsley, not pinkies.

Appetizers

Learning how to provide dinner guests with an introduction to your cooking style before launching headfirst into a main course is a significant milestone on the way to becoming an accomplished chef. This demonstrates one's knowledge of how contrasting components of a meal work together, as well as offering a variety of unique flavors. Making bruschetta, for instance, is a great way to start. Some apprentice Guidos may just scoop some pico de gallo onto some toast. This laziness will be noticed by any serious palate, especially if you leave your salsa sitting on the kitchen counter. All it takes to really own this form of hors d'oeuvre is chopping some fresh tomatoes with garlic, basil, olive oil, and vinegar before adding it to some toasted French bread. Your audience will certainly appreciate your desire to use fresh ingredients, as well as the time it took to concoct this item (which most likely exceeded the hours of all your studies throughout high school).

While bruschetta is a good opportunity for you to demonstrate your chops in the kitchen, all of your abilities will add up to moot if you can't make decent garlic bread. This side dish is as Italian as a Vespa that runs on pesto, so not being able to create something edible and delicious will make you undateable and probably a social pariah somewhere on the level of Danny Bonaduce. Assembling a good loaf of garlic bread isn't exactly brain surgery. The only rule of thumb that you really need to heed is: when all else fails, add more butter. This philosophy has worked wonders for great chefs such as Emeril Lagasse, Paula Deen, and Chef Boyardee. Adding enough garlic to ward off

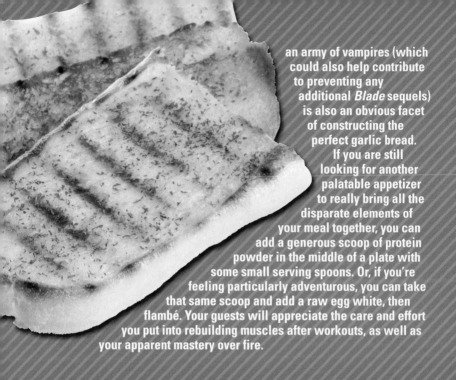

an army of vampires (which could also help contribute to preventing any additional *Blade* sequels) is also an obvious facet of constructing the perfect garlic bread. If you are still looking for another palatable appetizer to really bring all the disparate elements of your meal together, you can add a generous scoop of protein powder in the middle of a plate with some small serving spoons. Or, if you're feeling particularly adventurous, you can take that same scoop and add a raw egg white, then flambé. Your guests will appreciate the care and effort you put into rebuilding muscles after workouts, as well as your apparent mastery over fire.

Main Courses

When it comes to putting together an entrée, you basically want to craft a meal with all the thoughtfulness and restraint that go into the Girl Scout cookie recipes (seriously, more peanut butter and fudge?). But there are so many pastas and options for other foods out there, how do you choose a place to start? You should try to start small, striving for simplicity before biting off more than you can chew. Spaghetti and meat sauce is a perfect place to begin.

The pasta itself should be familiar enough, and preparation is minimal. All you need to do is bring a pot of water to a boil, toss the spaghetti in, then give it eight minutes to cook (this also offers Guidos a substantial amount of time to get in a set of push-ups, or for Guidettes to perform crucial hair maintenance). Adding a little olive oil and salt will help move the process along and lock in the flavor. You'll know the pasta is ready if you throw it against a fridge and it sticks. (NOTE: This is the same process that FOX uses to select its fall lineup.) Cultivating a savory meat sauce is another challenge entirely, however.

Composing a meat sauce is one of the more intimate things you can do in the kitchen, and how it turns out will be, in many ways, a reflection on your personality. The goal in this case should be not only to weave a variety of different spicy and sweet meats together, but also to clear out your shelves of spices that may have been sitting unused in your cabinets since 1998. This means basil, oregano, thyme, paprika, whatever (though you may want to go easy on the cinnamon). There's no secret formula for creating a delicious meat sauce; you'll find it really comes together after a great deal of trial and error. Having your friends sign nondisclosure agreements regarding the ingredients therein is also a smart move to maintain your recipe's secrecy without needing to embroil yourself in a potentially costly lawsuit.

Moving beyond pasta is another important milestone in your personal development, as it will let you spread your wings and try your hand at some other interesting dishes. Chicken cutlets will allow you to create an appetizing meal that is high in protein and low in fat—though certainly, you are well within your rights to douse every square inch of these meats with cheese and meat sauce. And heavy cream, of course. In fact, doing so will ensure that at the very least you'll have a meal so dense, you'll probably have to drop anchor while you're at the club later (everyone loves that guy). Sausage and peppers are also an essential comfort food to master, as these may be the only vegetables you've ever actually tried.

If you are going to make pizzas, please try to steer clear of the recipes of the major chains. Domino's originally perfected the "cardboard plus ketchup" recipe before they finally stopped insulting their customers. They now add two pinches of garlic to the cardboard and call it a day. As for Pizza Hut, they spent most of the 1990s and 2000s exploring different orifices of the pie in which to inject ever more cheese. (NOTE: Only a fat person would think of that.) These chefs are playing God, only

with mozzarella, Parmesan, and Gouda. If you truly want a classic Italian-style pizza, first you have to accept that it will be a thin-crust pizza. Not to disparage the deep-dish style that gained such popularity in places like Chicago, but these are more like tomato pies than anything else. If you can't fold a slice of pizza, you're holding an impostor. Once you've accepted this premise, you should strive for a pizza that uses a nice balance of sauce, cheese, and toppings,

so as not to overwhelm the palate. If you do decide to go heavy on any particular item, it never hurts to go heavy on the meat, creating a delicate blend of every cold cut under the sun. Once you've gone through two or three summer sausages and a log of pepperoni, you'll know you're on the right track. And remember, prosciutto is the new black.

Desserts

At the end of a delicious meal, you may occasionally have enough room left in your stomach to sample a nice end-of-the-meal treat from the motherland. In many cases, you can just prepare a cappuccino with biscotti, a nice pairing of a caffeine jolt and some of those celebrated twice-baked cookies. It's important to remember that a biscotti addiction can potentially sidetrack the muscular development that you've invested a great deal of time on at the gym. Empty calories are the number one threat to having a well-developed six-pack (narrowly edging out lack of body oil). If you can manage to limit your intake of these heavenly cookies, though, you will most likely find yourself satiated and content. And remember, if you really up the caffeine composition of the coffee you drink, you'll rocket your heart rate and metabolism into hyperdrive, which will help you melt away those precious ounces that dare defile your midsection.

Gelato is another sweet treat you can put together to cap a tasty dinner, which can provide a nice cooling sensation to offset the warmth of the main course. If you decide to make gelato, you should take great care to ensure that its sweetness provides a nice respite from the savory nature of the rest of the meal you've just concocted. If you are

able to come up with a finished product with the approximate sugar content of Fun Dip, you've done well. (NOTE: Fun Dip is perhaps one of the most amazing products of all time. You dip a stick of sugar . . . into more sugar! Given that backdrop, it's amazing that this country is such a teeming horde of fat asses. If you ever wonder why the nation is beset by methamphetamine addicts, video game junkies, and kids who pop Ritalin to control an ever-rampaging ADD epidemic, it may just be because we've run out of orifices to cram sugar into.)

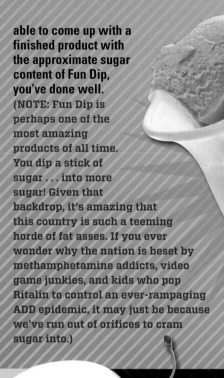

Drinks

Being able to craft a delicious cocktail is also an important part of any meal (or before hitting the town). You don't need to be a certified mixologist or anything, but you should strive to have a couple of tasty options for guests whenever the occasion calls for it. The first important piece of this puzzle is getting the right type (and volume) of alcohol. When it comes to the types of hard liquor you choose, it's really a lot less about the brands or kinds of alcohol that you select and more about the price. You're looking for cheap no-name brands of vodka, gin, whiskey, and tequila that are highly cost-effective, so you can leverage the ability to buy in bulk. Just remember, there is nothing worse

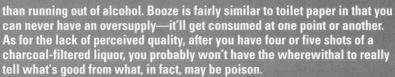

than running out of alcohol. Booze is fairly similar to toilet paper in that you can never have an oversupply—it'll get consumed at one point or another. As for the lack of perceived quality, after you have four or five shots of a charcoal-filtered liquor, you probably won't have the wherewithal to really tell what's good from what, in fact, may be poison.

Wines and beers are also a core element of the Guido experience. Though you don't need to possess the arcane knowledge of a sommelier, being able to tell the difference between white and red wine is pretty much a must. Your choice should come down to alcohol percentage and whether the contents of the bottle smell like carrion. As for beer, microbreweries have not been able to penetrate the landscape of the Jersey Shore as they have along the Pacific Coast and certain parts of Colorado. Much of this is due in fact to the lack of decent hops and barley available in the New Jersey area, often because arable land is usually dedicated to cultivating the nonchemical base elements for bronzer and hair gel. The beers that tend to be most popular tend to be the cheapest and most watered-down, given that the preferred method of consumption is funneling, shotgunning, and skulling cans as fast as possible.

Complications

Before diving into your optimal Guido diet, you should recognize that some of the items you cram down your gullet may not be the healthiest things in the world for you, and may cause some adverse reactions in your body. One potential drawback of a diet so laden with saturated fats and fatty lipids is that it's possible you will fart so much that you will start floating in place like the genie from *Aladdin*. The sheer volume of cheese that you consume also will probably have an unfavorable effect on your health, given that your arteries will begin to clog and your heart will begin to strain like a cement mixer. That, at least, needs to be on your periphery as you make your culinary selections.

Of course, it's not all about saturated fats and high cholesterol counts, but on the sheer volume of consumption in the first place. You should also carefully monitor your caloric intake; before you know it, you could look like one of the heifers grunting her way through the six thirty p.m. Cardio Rumble Stampede class at your local Curves gym. Not to say you can't live a happy, fulfilling life if you're a little bit on the heavy side, but not everyone is as fortunate as the chubby Kardashian (a.k.a. Gordo Kardo). If you maintain dedicated oversight over what goes into your body, you will enjoy a variety of delicious gastronomic choices, while not having to set up residence in your local gym.

Conclusion

In the Jersey Shore subculture, food and drink go beyond mere sustenance, and have a value that cannot simply be expressed in terms of calories and serving sizes. Along the long and winding road from hunter-gatherers to the present (and not all Guidos have evolved as readily as those from other tribes), preparing meals became an intricate part of the fabric of society. Sitting around the dinner table helped families and communities interact with one another, all while having the opportunity to break bread together. To do your part and continue this vibrant tradition, it's important to develop a handful of useful skills around the kitchen so you can tell the difference between a teaspoon and a tablespoon. Being able to subsist on nothing more than cheese, garlic, and olive oil is another impressive skill and should probably be the centerpiece of your résumé; it assures that you won't be reduced to foraging for stray pasta scraps in the street.

SUN'S OUT, GUNS OUT ... OR, OBTAINING THE ULTIMATE GUIDO TAN

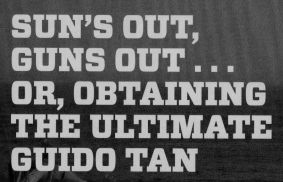

The Value of Tanning

While possessing a steroid-fueled granite exterior and maintaining the philosophy of a bonsai gardener regarding your hair and eyebrows are vital to fulfilling your destiny as a true Guido, all of these steps will be for naught if you're a whiter shade of pale. Basically, you're looking for a hue of orange that could not possibly occur in nature, similar to the flavors Gatorade has been churning out for the past twenty years. If you look like the bastard offspring of a

wild three-way between Garfield, a Creamsicle, and a tub of bronzer, you're good to go. Actually, a better descriptor would be the Orange Chicken at Panda Express, though the Sesame Chicken is also acceptable. (Note: Extra wonton not included.) Tanning should be a part of your daily routine, like lifting weights or not maintaining gainful employment. An integral part of the Guido Experience is not just going through the motions, but fully committing yourself. Just as getting on a NordicTrack just one time is basically meaningless, a tan here or there shows zero dedication. What you need is consistency. You wouldn't go a day without breathing, would you? Then why would you avoid giving your skin that healthy, eerie glow? Sure, your skin will have the texture of an old horse saddle in thirty years, but live in the here and now. A deep tan not only makes you look more vibrant, but it really helps define the muscles you're working so hard in the gym, as well as bringing out the intricate inkwork in your barbed-wire tattoo.

Guidettes, getting your skin to that optimal traffic-cone color is imperative. Your ultimate goal should be to take on all the characteristics of a basketball: orange, leathery, and constantly being groped by the hands of large men. The best way to bring out your fake boobs, drawn-on eyebrows, and tastefully done tramp stamp is a nice, healthy shade of tangerine. If you've already taken the time to wear a shirt that weighs less than thirteen microns or jeans so ripped that passersby can readily identify whether the carpet matches the drapes, then why would you settle for Conan O'Brien's skin tone? The only way a girl is realistically going to land the juiced-out

Guido of her dreams is if he looks at her and sees, in many ways, the mirror image of himself.

Location

An equally important part of choosing your tanning salon should be to size up the staff who work there. First of all, it is paramount that every employee look like a full-grown Oompa Loompa. It's important to know that they are confident enough and unintelligent enough to consistently utilize the product they sell. Second, your goal should be to choose a salon with a staff that will not, collectively, be able to field even a single one of your questions. This demonstrates a sun-bakedness that ensures that they not only are tanning during their breaks, but also may forget to charge you for tans once in a while, dollars that can be *immediately* reinvested into protein powder and Red Bull. Finally, if you can find a tanning salon that is adjacent to your gym or laundromat (or another place that takes up an inordinate part of your time), you can cut down on commuting time and really focus on bringing out that nice, healthy orange glow.

GYM *and* TAN
OPEN 24 HOURS

A couple of notes on general decorum and dress. You should attempt to adopt a minimalist philosophy when it comes to clothing, as the more you wear, the higher the incidence of unsightly tan lines. Clearly, the weapon of choice in terms of dress should be the banana hammock, which—although it will make you look as though you are smuggling grapes and other perishables over the border—covers the smallest amount possible, ensuring a healthy tan and conforming to most local statutes regarding public decency. To truly accentuate the tan, it is also highly recommended that your wardrobe choice be exclusively neon pink, neon green, or any color that was last popular in the 1980s. Guidettes, it is recommended that you wear something impossibly small that will undoubtedly bring great shame not only to your parents, but to at least three generations of relatives as well.

Lubrication

Beyond proper attire, it is imperative that you prepare your body properly to accept the pseudo sun's healing rays. It is highly recommended that you apply copious amounts of Hawaiian Tropic or other high-quality tanning lubricant prior to your session. Not only will these products provide you with a sickeningly sweet smell, sure to test the gag reflexes of all patrons within a twenty-foot radius, but your Crisco-oiled body will be primed like a Thanksgiving turkey. Anytime you can apply a term like "viscosity" to your person, that's a good thing. If you look like you've just gotten off shift at the Busty Beaver at three a.m. (NOTE: free wings during the K-Y Jelly wrestling show), then you are locked and loaded.

Music

While other tanning newbies may wish to pass the time listening to their iPods—I mean, that hard electro-house music ain't gonna listen to itself—there must be a word of caution when it comes to plugging in your earphones. First of all, that earbud cord, while infinitesimally thin, is still covering up some small part of you that is desperately yearning to be bronzed. That's a no-

go. Sure, it may just represent a small line from your waist to your ears, but the San Andreas Fault is just a small crack in the earth. It's this type of mistake that can stop you from going to the club and bringing home a ten, instead forcing you to bring back two fives. (NOTE: This is the worst kind of mathematical equation.)

If you must listen to music during your tanning session, avoid hard-core house music in favor of lighter fare. The reason for this is that it is effectively impossible to listen to Tiësto's latest essential mix without involuntary fist-pumping, which will limit your session's chromatic potential and could lead to harm of the actual tanning bed. In fiscal year 2008, approximately $438,346 in damages were accrued due to this series of events in tanning salons throughout New Jersey. Don't be part of the problem. Better options for your tanning session include Bon Jovi's "Slippery When Wet" (exceedingly likely), Bruce Springsteen's "Born to Run" (somewhat likely), Beethoven's Ninth Symphony (unlikely), or a wide assortment of books on tape (unfathomably unlikely).

Perfecting the Tan

It's perfectly normal to want to work your way up to a decent amount of time in the tanning bed. The first couple of experiences may seem jarringly unnatural and unsettling, but these are how you build up your tolerance to the tanning lights. Some have compared the whole experience, especially sliding into the oddly shaped bed, as "stepping into a time machine." This is completely accurate, assuming you've set the dials on the tanning bed to take you to Year Holy-Crap-You-Look-Fucking-Awesome. Remember, even if it feels uncomfortable at first, it is serving a valuable purpose, much like wearing a cast on a broken bone or wearing a condom with that woman of questionable scruples you just met in the alley of the club near the dumpster.

Once you've hit your tanning stride, it's important to determine how long you want your sessions to last. A good rule of thumb is to try to test the limits of what is medically safe and socially acceptable. Effectively, you should be pushing for a condition referred to as *Melanalmost*, which is the limit of what most HMO plans will allow you to purposely inflict on yourself before you are basically setting the dial on your bed to read "cancer." Interestingly enough, the value of a tan does not follow a linear path; rather, its awesomeness can be classified only as an exponential progression.

At a certain point, you may notice the wafting aroma of a delicious southern barbecue. Breathe in deeply, my friend—that is the smell of your charred flesh. It is at this juncture that your tan can go one of two divergent paths. You can settle for average, and look like every other juicehead on the dance floor. Or, you can go for something timeless and epic, that guy everyone will be talking about the next day (especially the latest Guidette you smooshed). It's just like working out: only pushing through the pain will get you the results you so desperately crave.

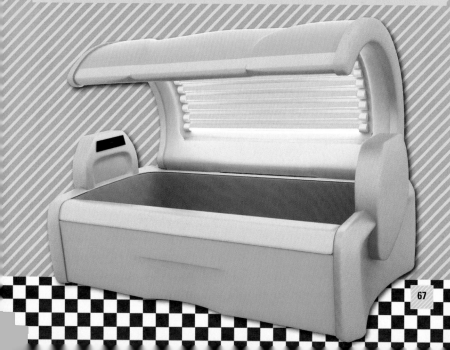

So go that extra mile to give yourself results that will last. Just remember, every freckle you see left on your body is God's way of saying, "Ten more minutes, chief."

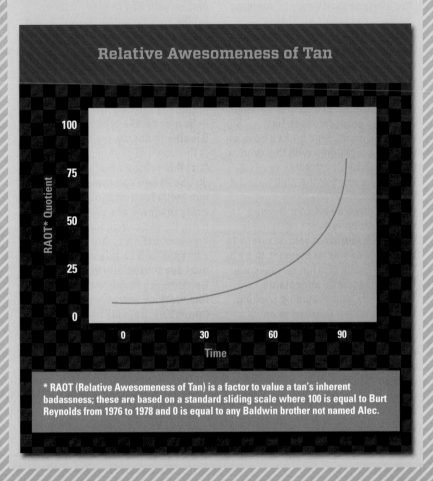

Relative Awesomeness of Tan

RAOT* Quotient

100
75
50
25
0

0   30   60   90

Time

* RAOT (Relative Awesomeness of Tan) is a factor to value a tan's inherent badassness; these are based on a standard sliding scale where 100 is equal to Burt Reynolds from 1976 to 1978 and 0 is equal to any Baldwin brother not named Alec.

Post-Tan Reflectionary Period (and Deep Thoughts)

Upon departing the tanning bed, it is important to follow standard protocols for exiting not only the apparatus, but the facility as well.

The first thing you should do is give yourself a once-over in a full-length mirror, in order to root out any dangerously insurgent tan lines that may seek to do damage to your stunning visage. This fairly simple task assures that you did not waste the last ninety minutes cranking on a tan that is, although ripping, still woefully short of perfect. These little touchups will take you from good to great.

It is also important to note that you must fulfill certain duties upon exiting the facility. It is standard practice to egregiously hit on the jailbait working the front desk and the smoothie bar. Additionally, you must look menacingly at males entering the establishment, just as a matter of course. Conversely, women leaving the salon should snidely comment on the lack of melanin present in any female within earshot. Also, you should probably wipe down your tanning bed to conform to local health and safety codes. That's just good manners.

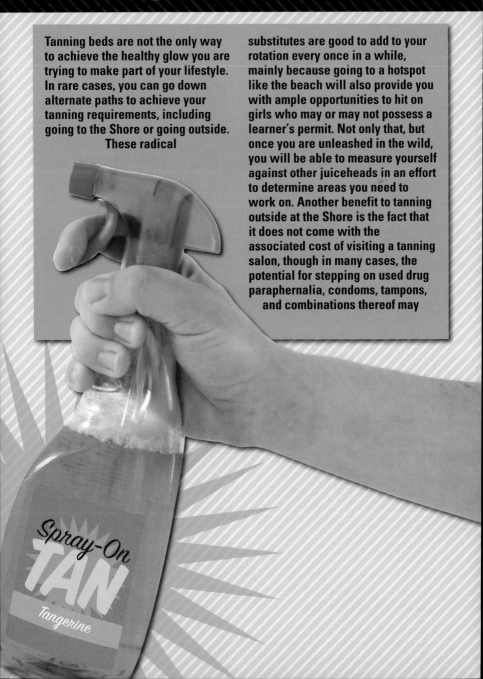

Tanning beds are not the only way to achieve the healthy glow you are trying to make part of your lifestyle. In rare cases, you can go down alternate paths to achieve your tanning requirements, including going to the Shore or going outside. These radical substitutes are good to add to your rotation every once in a while, mainly because going to a hotspot like the beach will also provide you with ample opportunities to hit on girls who may or may not possess a learner's permit. Not only that, but once you are unleashed in the wild, you will be able to measure yourself against other juiceheads in an effort to determine areas you need to work on. Another benefit to tanning outside at the Shore is the fact that it does not come with the associated cost of visiting a tanning salon, though in many cases, the potential for stepping on used drug paraphernalia, condoms, tampons, and combinations thereof may offset any potential cash savings.

The negative effects of tanning outdoors are visibly clear. Getting an even tan is more difficult and requires a great deal more time—time that could be spent doing sit-ups or creating potent new cocktails. The weather is a much greater issue. Outside or at the Shore, you're dealing with clouds and weather patterns. You shouldn't have to determine whether that cumulonimbus formation represents a potential threat to your tan's integrity. The fact of the matter is, you know what you're getting at a tanning salon. You go in, you pay your money, it's hyperefficient. If you must leave your epidermis to the fierce unpredictability of the elements, please bro, do so in moderation.

As for spray-tanning, that's like when Coca-Cola introduced New Coke, or Sammy Hagar took over for DLR in Van Halen. Sure, it may look or feel mildly similar to the original, but you're not fooling anybody. No purist can possibly accept the spray-on tan. At least getting inside a tanning bed simulates the actual act of lying out at the beach. A spray-on tan is administered by the same machines that provide Maaco paint jobs for your car at the reasonable price of $29.99. Why surrender your tan to the whims of a machine that is no further advanced than a bottle of Windex?

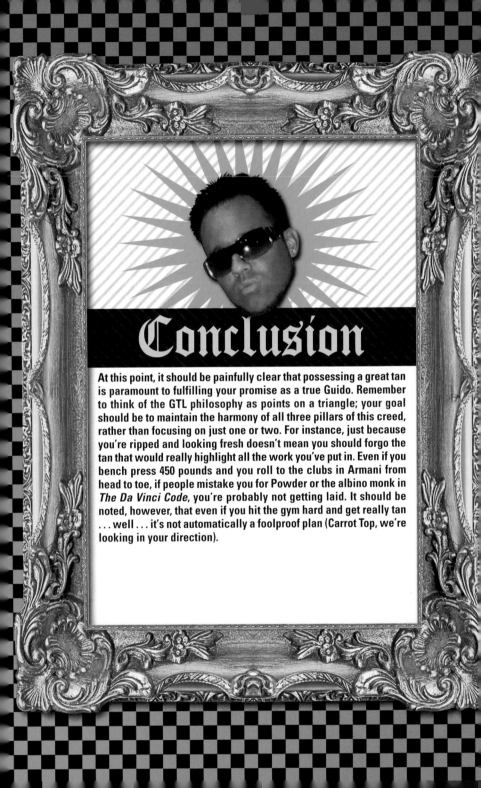

Conclusion

At this point, it should be painfully clear that possessing a great tan is paramount to fulfilling your promise as a true Guido. Remember to think of the GTL philosophy as points on a triangle; your goal should be to maintain the harmony of all three pillars of this creed, rather than focusing on just one or two. For instance, just because you're ripped and looking fresh doesn't mean you should forgo the tan that would really highlight all the work you've put in. Even if you bench press 450 pounds and you roll to the clubs in Armani from head to toe, if people mistake you for Powder or the albino monk in *The Da Vinci Code*, you're probably not getting laid. It should be noted, however, that even if you hit the gym hard and get really tan . . . well . . . it's not automatically a foolproof plan (Carrot Top, we're looking in your direction).

JERSEY INK . . . OR, TATS AND PIERCINGS

While a nice fake tan and frighteningly bloated muscles are core components of the Guido look, there is at least some degree of transience at play, and these solutions are always impermanent. Heck, even your hair is something that may start to thin and fade away, as though it were your bank account after a particularly unlucky weekend at the dog track. With beauty functioning as such a fleeting reflection of youth, you may start to wonder whether there is anything you can do to stem the tide. That is where the tattoo comes in. There's nothing like finding something that you care about, or can at least pretend to care about, then making it part of your exterior for the remainder of your life. Tattoos surged in popularity through much of the 1990s and 2000s, and became so ubiquitous in society that now it may seem like more of a rebellious act *not* to get that tattoo of Mighty Mouse stenciled mere inches from your pecker.

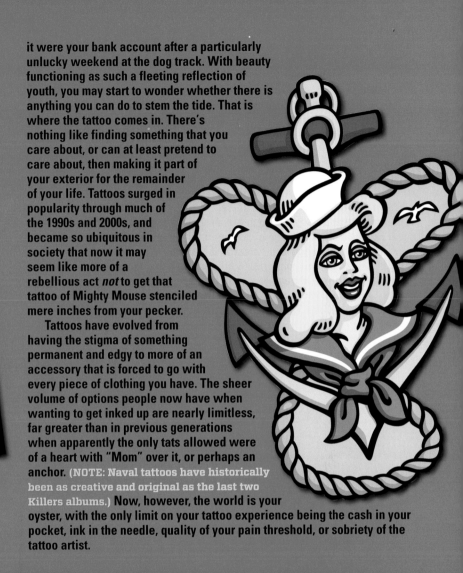

Tattoos have evolved from having the stigma of something permanent and edgy to more of an accessory that is forced to go with every piece of clothing you have. The sheer volume of options people now have when wanting to get inked up are nearly limitless, far greater than in previous generations when apparently the only tats allowed were of a heart with "Mom" over it, or perhaps an anchor. (NOTE: Naval tattoos have historically been as creative and original as the last two Killers albums.) Now, however, the world is your oyster, with the only limit on your tattoo experience being the cash in your pocket, ink in the needle, quality of your pain threshold, or sobriety of the tattoo artist.

Tattoos of Names

A fairly standard choice when it comes to getting a new tat is to opt for recording your name somewhere on your body. This is especially important in the fairly likely chance you forget it or on the off chance that you have to go to the hospital after a freak fist-pumping accident. Getting a name stenciled also allows you to leverage a wide variety of different fonts to make your newfound body art seem even more bad-ass, especially cursive or Gothic Old English.

It's fairly simple to just opt for your own name, and that helps you to build the sort of narcissistic self-actualization that is vital to your success. To take it to the next level, though, the most cutting-edge Guidos (NOTE: possible oxymoron) decide to get their nicknames carved onto their bodies. Given that these monikers are almost universally self-given, such tattoos represent the ultimate nexus of conceit and self-absorption. It's a beautiful thing. If you can find an artist who can tastefully write your nickname with flames shooting out the sides of the letters, you can stop looking. You've found your Da Vinci.

Beyond just your own name, though, it is always a good idea to get your significant other's name permanently etched on your body. That almost never comes back to haunt you, except for the decades and decades of overwhelming evidence to the contrary. If anything, though, getting a tattoo of a girl named Jen on your chest will just make you focus on dating future girls with that name, though you can also have a tattoo artist touch it up so it says "Jenga is a great game" or "Bruce Jenner was a great athlete." No one will be the wiser. They may just think you're weird or a tool. Or a weird tool.

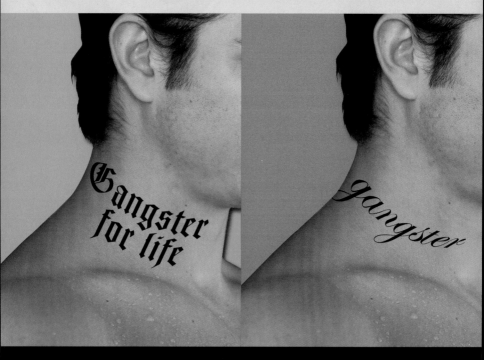

GOTHIC OLD ENGLISH   CURSIVE

Italian Heritage

Even if you are fourth- or fifth-generation Italian and are unable to locate Italy on a map (c'mon, it's a boot for crying out loud!), you must be steadfast in your celebration of all things Italian. Whether it's an oversized Italian flag draped on your wall or a slight accent or inflection that you throw into your speech patterns when you get worked up, it's these little things that will help solidify your entire persona. Being able to actually name a city or two in Italy is also a nice touch, though not essential.

While all of the above items or traits are great to have, they are missing the certain degree of finality and permanence that a well-placed tattoo can offer. In order to truly flex (and yes, "flex" is the operative word) your Italian heritage, it's important that you adorn your body with some sort of unmistakable reference to your motherland (again, this is appropriate even if you have never left the tri-state area). Guidos, the most common

variety of this self-expression takes place in the form of a giant Italian flag that encompasses roughly your entire back. Nothing says "I'm Eye-talian" more than a flag tattoo that takes up more room than John Goodman in a phone booth. The tricolor alone will be proof of your dedication, as the intricate needlework will undoubtedly cause you a great deal of pain. It's a small price to pay for eternal grandeur.

There are several other distinctive methods to let everyone know your background. Some of the most obvious examples include getting Italian phrases inked onto highly visible segments of your body. These can include *Acqua cheta rovina i ponti* (Still waters run deep), *L'amore è bello* (Love is beautiful), and *Dovresti averlo controllato* (You should get that checked out). And of course, nothing beats a tat that screams "Italian Stallion" from either your forearm or your chest. If you pair the words with an actual drawing of a horse, no one will dare think of giving you shit ever again (mainly because it's hard to pick a fight with someone when you're laughing uncontrollably). Any of these options will represent your ancestors appropriately, assuming of course that you don't mind them continually rolling in their graves from your latest ill-conceived exploits.

ITALIAN CITY CHEAT SHEET

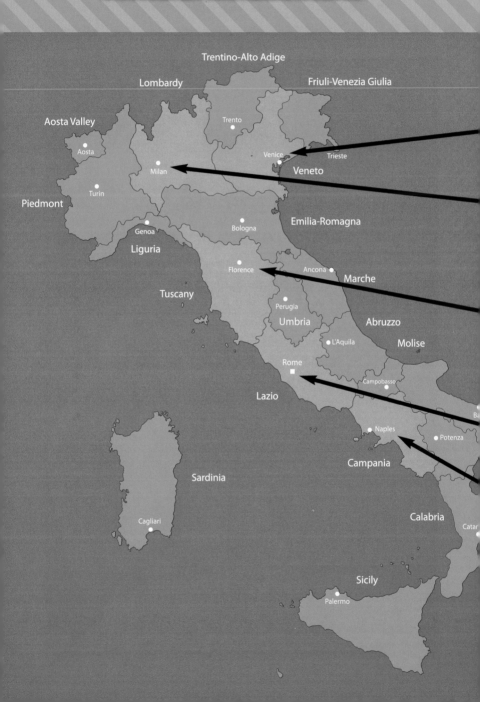

VENICE

The "City of Water" is renowned for the canals which flow through its buildings. Venice has long been considered one of the world's most romantic cities, slightly edging out Trenton, New Jersey.

MILAN

One of the famed locations of global fashion, considered in the same sentence as New York, Paris, and Tokyo. Probably not the type of place you would find a preponderance of Ed Hardy shirts.

FLORENCE

The most populous city in Tuscany, Florence was the center of much development during the Renaissance. The city was birthplace of the writer Machiavelli, who you may know from reading *The Prince* (really?) or listening to 2Pac (that's more like it).

ROME

The capital of Italy and birthplace of an inordinate amount of cultural landmarks. The famed Coliseum will even remind passersby of the movie *Gladiator*, which totally kicked ass and spawned the porn movie "Glad He Ate Her" joke, which is just fantastic.

NAPLES

One of the more populous areas of Italy, Naples is home to delicious pizza and has rebuilt itself after being the most bombed Italian city in World War II. The city's name also sounds like "nipples," which is pretty awesome.

Religious Emblems

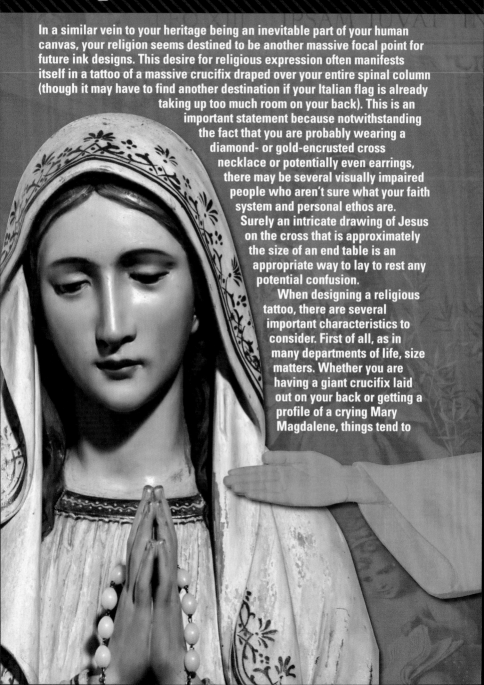

In a similar vein to your heritage being an inevitable part of your human canvas, your religion seems destined to be another massive focal point for future ink designs. This desire for religious expression often manifests itself in a tattoo of a massive crucifix draped over your entire spinal column (though it may have to find another destination if your Italian flag is already taking up too much room on your back). This is an important statement because notwithstanding the fact that you are probably wearing a diamond- or gold-encrusted cross necklace or potentially even earrings, there may be several visually impaired people who aren't sure what your faith system and personal ethos are. Surely an intricate drawing of Jesus on the cross that is approximately the size of an end table is an appropriate way to lay to rest any potential confusion.

When designing a religious tattoo, there are several important characteristics to consider. First of all, as in many departments of life, size matters. Whether you are having a giant crucifix laid out on your back or getting a profile of a crying Mary Magdalene, things tend to have more impact if they take up ridiculous swathes of territory. Your goal should be to create a design that is rich in meaning and subtlety, then magnify it four or five times so it fills an entire body part, thus removing any shred of subtlety that may previously have existed. This is a tried and true formula that has worked for a variety of people throughout history in other avenues, most notably Stone Temple Pilots and any actor from the cast of *Friends* (sorry, Schwimmer).

A very popular phrase that can also adorn your body while conveying your innermost faith is "Only God can judge me" (OGCJM). This is a great choice for you to consider because it basically allows you to do whatever you'd like with impunity, since you are no longer subject to the rules of man. There's nothing like demonstrating your fervent belief in Catholicism while also expressing your lack of consideration for the general principles of cause and effect. While this is a great way to demonstrate an infuriating sense of entitlement on the level of Spencer from *The Hills*, you may notice some drawbacks to whether OGCJM is applicable in real-life examples. It may be surprising to know that, besides the fact that your peers will undoubtedly and constantly be judging you, your actions and behavior will certainly be critiqued by the Seaside Heights Police Department, most likely to your detriment.

Tribal Designs

Surely at some point over the last two decades, you've seen a guy at the gym (without sleeves, of course) who had some sort of weird, unidentifiable pattern on his shoulder. This intricate webbing of generic unoriginality is impressive not only because it often takes up massive amounts of real estate on a body, but because the meanings of the designs are frequently lost on the actual owners of said art (this is very similar in many regards to folks who get Chinese characters tattooed on their shoulders, only to find out years later that the scrawlings were not originally quoted by Confucius). In many cases, it can be a cheaper and quicker solution to have a five-year-old with ADD provide your design, as it will be at least a stone's throw from what a professional would charge you hundreds of dollars for.

When you choose a tribal armband, it's important to use a blueprint that is as confusing as possible to the naked eye; you don't want to constantly have to explain what it is: a veritable kudzu of fail. It's much easier to deal with stunned silence and a variety of friends and onlookers who will never wonder what the artwork signifies (or God forbid, what tribe it is from) in fear that you will launch into some meandering diatribe to explain its relevance. The beauty of this styling is in its simplicity; there is no room for color variation, which really allows your tattoo artist to focus on just how muddled and ludicrous this convoluted design will be. And remember one important tenet: anytime you can rock a style that was beaten into the ground and fucked out ten years ago, you have to grab that bull by the horns.

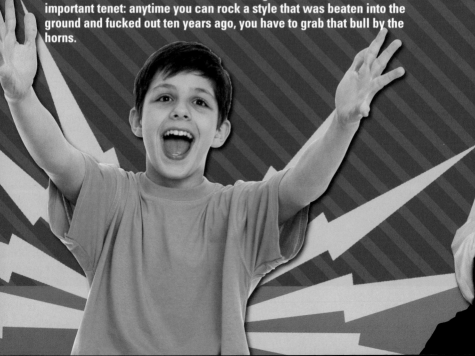

Tramp Stamps

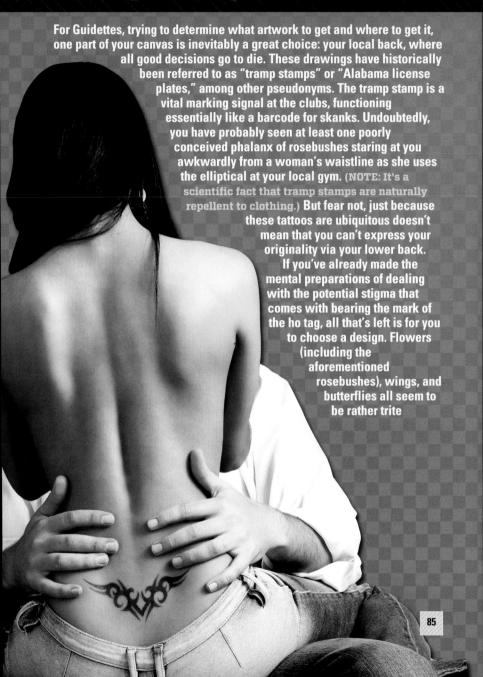

For Guidettes, trying to determine what artwork to get and where to get it, one part of your canvas is inevitably a great choice: your local back, where all good decisions go to die. These drawings have historically been referred to as "tramp stamps" or "Alabama license plates," among other pseudonyms. The tramp stamp is a vital marking signal at the clubs, functioning essentially like a barcode for skanks. Undoubtedly, you have probably seen at least one poorly conceived phalanx of rosebushes staring at you awkwardly from a woman's waistline as she uses the elliptical at your local gym. (NOTE: It's a scientific fact that tramp stamps are naturally repellent to clothing.) But fear not, just because these tattoos are ubiquitous doesn't mean that you can't express your originality via your lower back. If you've already made the mental preparations of dealing with the potential stigma that comes with bearing the mark of the ho tag, all that's left is for you to choose a design. Flowers (including the aforementioned rosebushes), wings, and butterflies all seem to be rather trite

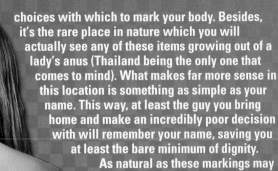

choices with which to mark your body. Besides, it's the rare place in nature which you will actually see any of these items growing out of a lady's anus (Thailand being the only one that comes to mind). What makes far more sense in this location is something as simple as your name. This way, at least the guy you bring home and make an incredibly poor decision with will remember your name, saving you at least the bare minimum of dignity.

As natural as these markings may be for Guidettes, the occasional times they are seen on the male version of the species represent significant cause for concern. Guidos, there is never any conceivable reason for you to get a tattoo of anything on your lower back. That is a region where masculinity goes to die and should be treated as such. You could get a design of Clint Eastwood fighting a bear with a lightsaber and it would look effete. Keep that in mind before making any potentially horrendous wagers with your friends that may involve you getting inked where your manhood will constantly be called into question.

Unique Piercings

Among women, you'll see piercings on every part of the body, both north and south of the equator. A region that has shown particularly impressive growth lately is the belly button. This has manifested itself not only in the simple, classic belly button ring, but also in the increasingly popular belly chain. These pieces of equipment can often be confused for fishing tackle

or the chandeliers that are used inside dollhouses, and are designed to be shiny enough to secure a Guido's undivided attention at twenty paces. It should be noted, however, that you should be in fairly good shape to pull one of these trinkets off successfully. If you have a little bit of a gut, there's a good chance you will look like your stomach is impersonating Wilford Brimley with a diamond mustache. Apologies if that made you throw up a little in your mouth.

Guidos generally have far more limited options when it comes to a unique piercing location, with one notable exception: the cock ring (a.k.a. the Prince Albert). In the U.S., roughly 45 percent of all Prince Albert piercings are in the Guido community. The cock ring per capita (CRPC) rates within one hundred miles of the Jersey Shore are off the charts, and span an impressive range of baubles. Some of these piercings are the essence of simplicity, with only a ring or stud to speak of. At the other end of the spectrum, the higher-end piercings have such intricate facets that they can be mistaken for a high school class ring, high-end chandelier, or a Christmas ornament (except, you know, it's on your penis).

Tattoo Removal

While more often that not, you will wear your ink with pride, occasionally an area on your body may provide a ringing reminder of how a potent amount of alcohol can have a deleterious effect on your decision-making skills. All is not lost, however. With the growth in the number of tattoos, the prevalence of facilities designed to remove them has risen as well. The advent of laser ink-removal facilities meant that in the unfortunate case that your Bell Biv DeVoe tattoo would someday cease to be relevant, several short hours of agonizing pain would remove the etchings of a misspent youth.

The beauty of this process is revealed in its intricate circle of life. You choose a design, you get inked up, and somewhere down the road, you may choose to get it removed, leaving your skin barren as it once was. The only difference is that in the aftermath of this laser removal, your epidermis will take on a leathery, scorched-earth quality. Also, the whole process will generally cost you several hundred dollars for the original tattoo and several thousand to press your body's version of Control-Alt-Delete. At the very least, you'll probably get to read some issues of *Highlights* from 1996 in the waiting room.

Conclusion

The landscape of the Guido is constantly in flux and ever-changing. Nowhere is this more apparent than in the types of tattoos which males and females of the species choose as lasting marks on the temples that are their bodies. The locations of these human graffiti and the topics that generally are the core components of this Guido artwork—fervent Italian pride, effusive demonstration of anything and everything Catholic, and constant reminders of the wearer's name and alias—are all vital elements as you build yourself Guido from the ground up. All you need to remember is this: nearly everything you choose to decorate your body with will be inherently ridiculous, so just do your best and make sure you do a spell check beforehand or you'll invariably wind up looking like a jackass.

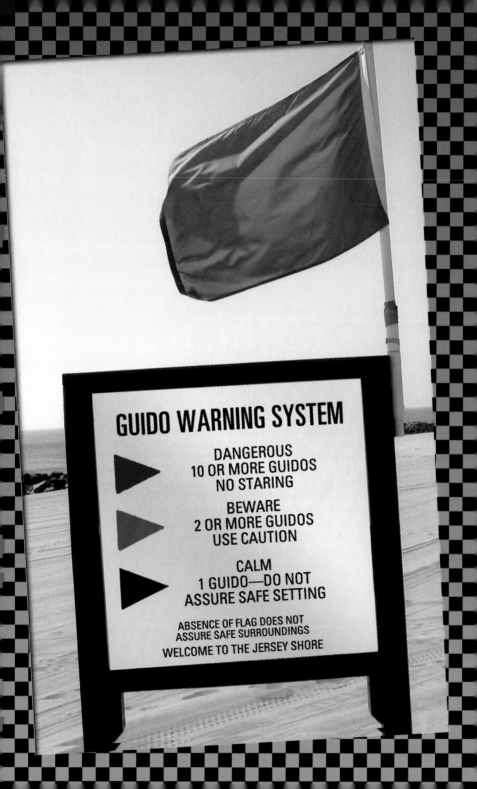

TO BLOWOUT OR NOT TO BLOWOUT . . . OR, THE ART OF GETTING ONE'S HAIR DID

A critical element of the Guido and Guidette mosaic is how hair is coiffed, styled, and presented. The only limit to the ridiculousness you can achieve with your hairstyle is your own imagination. Your hair goes beyond simply choosing a style, though. You also want to make sure you've got a routine in place for when you need to make the necessary touchups, and you know which products to turn to in order to make sure your look is held solidly in place.

Choosing a hairstyle is one of the more important things you will do in your lifetime, on the level of your first marriage and the birth of your children. (NOTE: Which order they rank in is up to you.)

Undoubtedly, many times the style will be a manifestation of the scalp you were blessed with. Guys with egg-shaped heads will probably tend to opt for blowouts because closely cropped cuts will only magnify how misshapen their skulls are. Similarly, women who have difficulties sculpting their bangs will probably steer clear of developing the poof. As is generally the case with the Guido and Guidette mindset, it's best not to overthink it.

Blowouts

Perhaps the most famous of all Guido hairstyles is the blowout. If you are having difficulty envisioning what this style looks like, add some water to your hand and pull your hair as high as it can possibly go. If you feel like you've started to pull some follicles out at the roots, you're probably headed in the right direction. While similar hairstyles in other youth cultures may advocate a slightly more subtle type of gel dispersal (e.g., the commonly seen "front frat flip," now exclusively available at every school in the Big Ten), it's not a true blowout unless you go for the gusto. Excess is your best friend in this situation. Devotees will carry around pocket rulers in order to ensure not only that they have maximum strand length (four to six inches is generally preferred), but that great care and consideration has been paid to uniformity throughout the scalp. The ruler may also be valuable for ensuring that those "pills" you ordered from the mail-order catalog are having their desired effects.

The best method for the initial stages of construction of a blowout is the base layer of gel. In many ways, this is like setting the foundation for a large residential high-rise community. By taking the time to guarantee strong support at the root level, you will ultimately strengthen the end product and avoid any messy gel-related lawsuits. (NOTE: The dual class-action

From there, it's a pretty simple process really—just spread your fingers like you're palming a basketball, turn them over, douse with styling product, and push upward through your hair. You will know you are doing it right if people consistently confuse you with a backup dancer for Lady Gaga. It's the price you pay for looking good.

Once you've pushed your hair to limits that seem to refute many of the basic tenets of Newtonian physics, it's time to meticulously go through and determine that every strand of hair has been given the same game plan. You don't want to wait in line at the club for forty-five minutes, only to realize that two hairs three-eighths of an inch behind your right ear have been smothered under a globule of mousse. That's the type of thing that every discerning Guidette (OK, only about 9 percent of them have any discriminating standards) will be able to sniff out in a heartbeat and move on to the next juicehead. To avoid this potential pitfall, bust out your magnifying mirror and begin the crucial process of "follicle socialism," slowly indoctrinating each hair with a unifying message: look awesome.

Women at the Shore historically react very positively to this hairstyle, and the alpha male of a particular group of potential Guido mates is almost inevitably whoever possesses the most stellar blowout. In many ways, the height of your hair is a surrogate for your virility, and you want your hair to look like a guy holding a hair dryer in a bathtub. To this end, it's important that you take the time to cultivate the style properly and

make sure that every woman within earshot understands the amount of time it takes you to look so alluring. Women respect a man who spends three to four hours doing his hair, especially if it keeps them from using the bathroom. That will in no way be a source of future discord.

Beyond the sheer value of looking incredible, you may notice that having an incredible blowout offers you many advantages over and above simple sex appeal. Random people on the street may start asking you to take photos with them. People may mistake you for the guy in those old Maxell commercials. Your titanium shell will also provide great shelter in the case of inclement weather. And let us not forget: another ancillary benefit of the 'do is that in case of potential altercations on the boardwalk, the style is very reminiscent of triceratops horns, which can be used to charge and subdue would-be aggressors, further solidifying your dominance of the herd.

Other Major Male Hairstyles

Sometimes you just need to face facts and understand that the blowout is not for you. You may be there in spirit, but you also have to have the hair to make it happen. Sometimes nature and desire do not conspire. Fret not, there are a variety of other classic Guido staples for you to choose from, each more ridiculous than the last. An example of this would be the tight fade, where all the effort really just goes into choosing a setting on your clippers. (NOTE: Every true Guido will own at least one pair of clippers, as well as a travel set.) The recommendation here is that you roll with a one or two and just go to town on your entire scalp, leaving it just a little bit longer on the top. There's not a whole lot more that goes into a sick fade, just attentiveness. You will want to make sure you're trimming every several days to ensure maximum freshness. If your single-minded focus on your fade blooms into full-scale OCD that would make Howard Hughes, Howie Mandel, or the host from *Double Dare* blush, you've done your duty.

Another classic look that you'll have at your disposal is today's version of the "faux hawk." This style maintains a lot of similarities to original

NOT THE FAUX

punk-rock-style Mohawks, except that it's typically shorter and does not require the subject to shave his head surrounding his center spikes. You will want to maintain a fairly tight crop on the rest of your scalp, though, or you risk being lumped together with the hairstyles of David Beckham, Adam Levine, and whatever other celebrity du jour wanted to immediately tell you about his 'do on his Twitter account (LOL!). Other names for this approach include the "bro-hawk," the "douche-ridge," and the "prick-crest."

THE FAUX

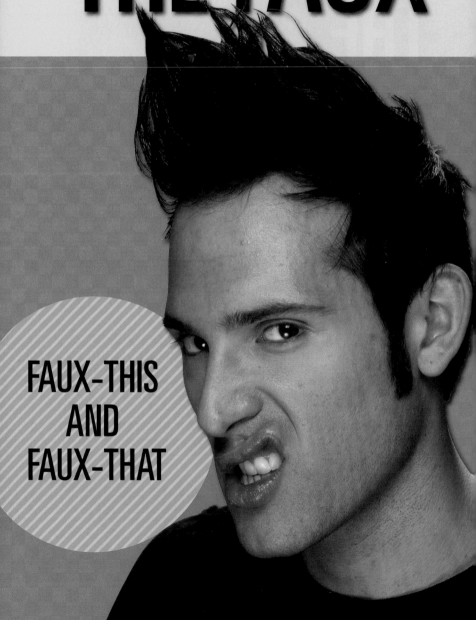

FAUX-THIS
AND
FAUX-THAT

GREAT SALON FIGHTS IN MODERN HISTORY

1995:

After Maria Tribonace received her semi-annual poof touch-up, she gets into an all-out brawl with Teresa Cinqueterra, who Maria claims has infringed upon her hair's copyright. In the subsequent melee, twelve poofs are destroyed and four industrial-strength vats of gel are rendered unusable. The case would be settled in small claims court for $235.16 within a year and a half.

2002:

Jenni Daulerio and Samantha Delmonico stage what is still being referred to as "The Mother of All Catfights." This brawl began at the Shear Perfection on Ocean Avenue before spilling out into the parking lot, ultimately ending up at the Long John Silver's. Daulerio claimed victory after ripping out a Teddy Ruxpin-sized chunk of Delmonico's hair. The cause of the spat is still being determined.

2009:

A visibly intoxicated Debbie Mazzeri goes into her local hair salon (whose name has been omitted due to the still-pending charges) looking to have a conversation with a hairdresser whom she believes is sleeping with her serious boyfriend of three weeks. What ensued was five broken hairdryers, three sets of scissors being used outside their suggested use, and a statewide restraining order. In addition to the women affected by Mazzeri's onslaught, two of the chairs at the salon have been named as plaintiffs on the pending class-action suit, due to damages incurred.

Poofs

Any discussion of the countless ways to coif one's hair would certainly be remiss without focusing on several palatable options for Guidettes out there. The "poof" hairstyle is akin to a female version of the blowout (originally titled the fem-blow; this term was barred from most credible hair salons in 1987), in which you are essentially trying to create some sort of optical illusion where your hair poofs up in the front. If you are having problems visualizing it, just think of a tanner, female, less vampirical version of the dude from Bram Stoker's *Dracula*.

The way to really go about building the underpinnings of a poof is to make sure you're using a shampoo that gives you more volume. Using a variety of different shampoos and conditioners will assist you in thickening your hair, as well as reaching your stated goal of spending an inordinate amount of your disposable income on beauty products. Before you turn to your trusty 1,200-volt hair dryer, you should take this volumizing process straight to the roots as well. Now that your hair is fuller than a fat kid after his fourth box of

Thin Mints, it's really just a matter of locking in your look. After two or three bottles of hairspray, you should have no problem locking in that absurd, comely bump in your hair. Sure, this reliance on aerosol products may contribute to a gigantic hole in the ozone layer, but Australia will thank you later once they're rocking those fantastic year-round tans. You're welcome, mates.

If you are unwilling to put in this level of effort and dedication for the best poof on the Shore, there is an alternative path. Certain drugstores sell hair care products called Bumpits (and other associated brands) that can be inserted underneath your hair to create the illusion of additional volume. While this may be a quick and easy solution that avoids the hours of prep time associated with more conventional routes, just remember that you are outsourcing your beauty needs to CVS and Walgreens. Sure, they may have helped every sad sack and/or ironic asshole in America get their hands on a Snuggie, but the product they were working with wasn't exactly the toast of Milan Fashion Week. To put Bumpits in another light: if this were elementary school, using these products would peg your coolness somewhere between the kid who ate his own boogers and the kid who smelled like a mixture of cottage cheese and farts. Take the time and effort to make your poof as God intended.

THE POOF

POOF-THIS
AND
POOF-THAT

Extensions

Sometimes Guidettes will find that they are just not happy with the quality or quantity of hair that God gave them. Hair quality is an item easily addressed by the aforementioned mountain of beauty products that will undoubtedly function in your house as a roommate that avoids paying rent. Hair quantity can be a much more vexing issue to solve for many Guidettes out there, though there are solutions.

Buying hair extensions can be a serious moral conundrum. Amazingly enough, there are some women who will gladly fake and bake, or have implants the size of bocce balls zipped inside their chest cavity, who would actually balk at the prospect of weaving fake hair into their scalp. This makes as much sense as an irritating yuppie who professes to hate publicly traded companies, yet happily pours three cups of Starbucks down his gullet every day. (NOTE: This describes approximately one-third of San Franciscans.) Once you can mentally accept the fact that extensions can be a wonderful contributor to a new look, it's time to choose some that work for you.

There are a multitude of different colors and styles available for your extensions, which will all have distinct ramifications. Choosing a set that blends nicely with your current hair color will help you

achieve that desired look of volume, and no one will be the wiser. That is, until you snag one of them on the coat rack after your twelfth Jack and Coke in yet another orgy or bout of poor decision-making. That is neither here nor there, though. If you truly want a look that encapsulates pure class, it is highly recommended that you get extensions that are the mirror-opposite color of your natural hair. This means if you're a blonde, go with black, or vice versa. You might remember this style being effectively popularized by Christina Aguilera during her "I'm a tramp who will ultimately regret this clear affront to my legacy" period.

Getting Your Hair Did

For Guidos, trips to barber salons are like a religious experience of their own. You can find one of these institutions in every community, and beyond the value of the cutting and styling, these situations are ripe for ball-busting. While you may ask yourself what the point is of going to a barber when all hairstyles can effectively be created with two to three minutes of your own time, sitting in a chair focusing on your hair with your friends can foster a sense of camaraderie that is unparalleled in other settings. Conversation that initially centers on each other's unique styles will soon shift to other amusing topics, such as the skank you brought home last night, your penchant for putting too much garlic in your meat sauce, or the skank you brought home last night. As you'll see in our subsequent chapter on male relationship cultivation, these interactions are unequivocally valuable.

The Guidos have their own traditions and customs when it comes to maintaining a top-quality hairstyle. Stylists will typically be able to recommend a number of different options for poof optimization, as well as help you tease out areas that give you more trouble than *People's* crossword puzzle. As they do for the fellas, trips to the hair salon help promote a spirit of togetherness between Guidettes, at least until the conversation ultimately takes an unfortunate turn, in which both Guidettes realize they've been with the same Guido concurrently. These arguments have led to the nearly 240 percent rise in scissor-related crimes since 1994.

Maintaining Your Look

Now that you have all the puzzle pieces together when it comes to choosing a great hairstyle that will get you more ass than a toilet seat, it's critical to devote a great deal of your time to cultivating and shaping your look. To this end, it's assumed that you will have to rely heavily on gel and hairspray products to construct hairstyles that may flout certain laws of physics and general social acceptance: gravity-defying blowouts, poofs that look like the cresting wave of a powerful tsunami, and fades that are so uniform down to the one-sixteenth of an inch that you might confuse them with a putting green at the Masters.

Guidos, there are a lot of different products you can use to really lock in the look you are going for. You may notice while purchasing some sort of gel-based product from your local bodega that nearly every brand will have some derivation of "super," "mega," or "ultra." The best recommendation in this case is to choose a product that combines most of these adjectives into a completely over-the-top name like Super-Mega-Ultra Hold. What you're aiming for is a product that sounds as though it was named by the same people who create Japanese game shows. If it sounds ridiculous, it's the product for you.

Given the sheer volume of gel that is prevalent throughout the Jersey Shore, initial discussions have begun regarding the region's qualifications as a potential member of OPEC. (NOTE: Saudi Arabia, Qatar, and the UAE are expected to announce their final decision in mid-2012.)

The close proximity to dozens of petrochemical plants in the northern New Jersey area represents a nice marriage between supply and demand. At any given time within the U.S., approximately 18 percent of all hair gel products are

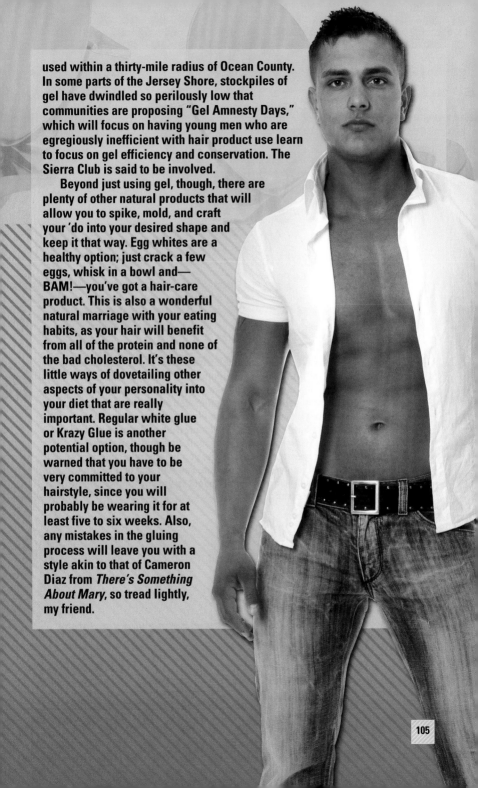

used within a thirty-mile radius of Ocean County. In some parts of the Jersey Shore, stockpiles of gel have dwindled so perilously low that communities are proposing "Gel Amnesty Days," which will focus on having young men who are egregiously inefficient with hair product use learn to focus on gel efficiency and conservation. The Sierra Club is said to be involved.

Beyond just using gel, though, there are plenty of other natural products that will allow you to spike, mold, and craft your 'do into your desired shape and keep it that way. Egg whites are a healthy option; just crack a few eggs, whisk in a bowl and—BAM!—you've got a hair-care product. This is also a wonderful natural marriage with your eating habits, as your hair will benefit from all of the protein and none of the bad cholesterol. It's these little ways of dovetailing other aspects of your personality into your diet that are really important. Regular white glue or Krazy Glue is another potential option, though be warned that you have to be very committed to your hairstyle, since you will probably be wearing it for at least five to six weeks. Also, any mistakes in the gluing process will leave you with a style akin to that of Cameron Diaz from *There's Something About Mary*, so tread lightly, my friend.

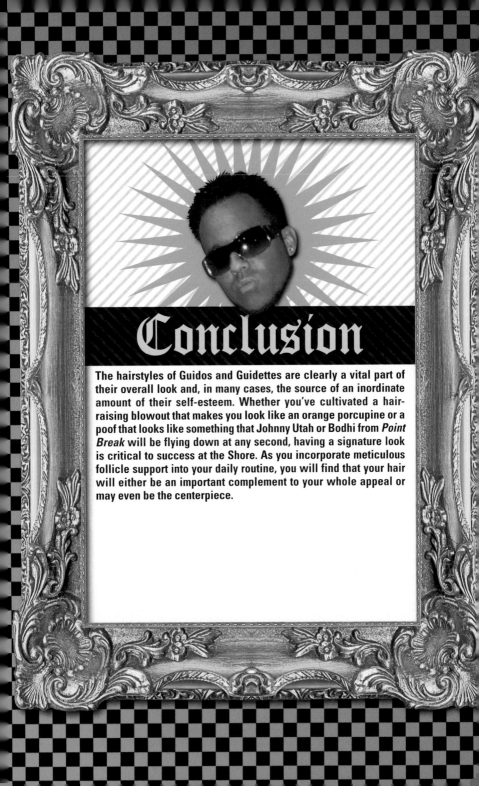

Conclusion

The hairstyles of Guidos and Guidettes are clearly a vital part of their overall look and, in many cases, the source of an inordinate amount of their self-esteem. Whether you've cultivated a hair-raising blowout that makes you look like an orange porcupine or a poof that looks like something that Johnny Utah or Bodhi from *Point Break* will be flying down at any second, having a signature look is critical to success at the Shore. As you incorporate meticulous follicle support into your daily routine, you will find that your hair will either be an important complement to your whole appeal or may even be the centerpiece.

NIP, TUCK, REPEAT . . . OR, CALF IMPLANTS, STEROIDS, AND EVERYTHING IN BETWEEN

Clearly, it's more important than ever to look your best at all times. With the advent of HDTV, flip cams, and videos getting uploaded to YouTube constantly, there is more pressure than ever to put your best foot forward. If you are even remotely famous, chances are you have a regular segment on *TMZ* or there is a potentially damaging sex tape of you making the

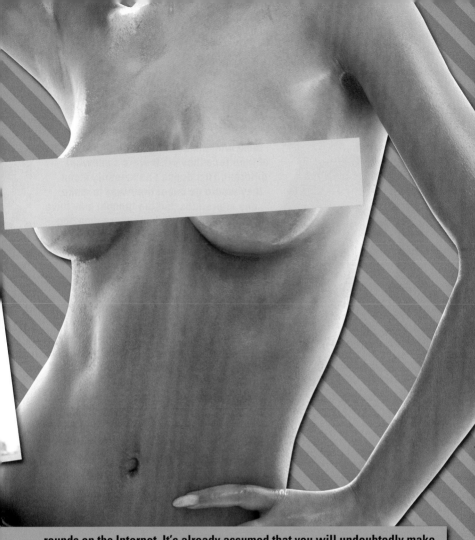

rounds on the Internet. It's already assumed that you will undoubtedly make an ass of yourself and bring great shame to your family, but shouldn't you at least look fantastic while you're doing it?

Plastic surgery can be a very divisive topic, and there are many moral and ethical quandaries that must be explored before making such a momentous decision. Plus, you can make your boobs really, really big. Realistically, though, any operations you get represent a massive investment and may lead you down a never-ending path where surgery feels like your only option. If this is confusing in any way, please see Joan Rivers from 1977 to the present. Beyond just the cost and the personal sentiments that go into these procedures, though, there really is no shortage of areas where you can nip, tuck, augment, remove, or generally treat your body as some real-time Mr. Potato Head experiment gone terribly awry.

Most women, Guidette or not, have a part of their face they wish were somewhat different. This doesn't necessarily mean they would go out of their way to make any alterations, but the thought may have crossed their minds. In these amazing times we live in, though, medical advances have come further than many medical school dropouts ever thought possible. Nowadays, there are a myriad of areas on your face that you can address individually—your eyes, skin, nose, lips, etc.—or you can just get the whole works done all at once (also known as the Donatella Versace or the Double Pelosi). A word of caution if you choose the latter route, however: though technology has caught up, Mother Nature is still undefeated, and there is at least an 80 percent chance you will end up looking like a combination of Dyan Cannon and Skeletor.

Eyes

They say the eyes are the windows to the soul. So wouldn't you pay a contractor who is good with windows to double-pane that shit? The same theoretical principles are in play. Good doctors will be able to provide you with a variety of different options when it comes to making your eyes more alluring. (NOTE: While none of this will actually improve your vision, anything purported to have actual value is immaterial to this discussion.) Focusing on budding crow's feet and wrinkles near your eyes will help take years off your age.

This is especially important if you're twenty-four and want to look like a slutty high school student, which has the dual value of allowing you to play a fun role and appealing directly to the more lascivious elements of Guido desire. This ability to directly "manage" your appearance and age also allows you to continue unabated with your terrible habits like staying up drinking until seven a.m. or smoking so many cigarettes that the Marlboro Man would sheepishly loan you some of his Nicorette. That, and your brighter eyes, may help you land a coveted lead role in an anime movie.

Cosmetic eyelid surgery is another valuable procedure. In other words, the puffy eyes that you accrued from absurdly unhealthy drinking sessions will be able to be attacked with the help of a board-certified doctor, or at the very least, by a professional who performs procedures eighteen miles out to sea (where the convoluted U.S. health care regulations do not apply). If there is any downside to this procedure, it's the fact that you will look as perpetually perky as a sales associate at Abercrombie & Fitch cruising around after three espressos. The end result may also make your skin as taut as a trampoline, where one errant glance could lead to total epidermal failure at any moment. But any time you can have some work done that could potentially lead to your tear ducts opening and closing seemingly at their own whim, you've got to do it.

For members of both sexes who may be looking for a procedure that may actually produce some sort of health benefits and potentially even improve the quality of life, you can go down the route of many people around the world and opt for laser eye surgery. This will enable you to see clearly without the aid of eyeglasses or contact lenses, which is especially helpful if you keep confusing energy drinks with your contact lens fluid. (NOTE: If this is the case, you may note lower levels of taurine and guarana after the procedure.) Regardless, you will note immense benefits from laser eye surgery, such as the ability to determine the amount of oregano you are using in a recipe down to the microgram, as well as determining exactly which hue you want to aim for at the tanning salon. Your vision will be so exact that you'll be able to pick out colors like they're Ralph Lauren paint samples.

Nose

Your nose may be another area you wish to address. Whether you've got an indentation on the bridge, widened nostrils, or a deviated septum, you should begin to realize that the appearance of your nose is paramount. Breathing and keeping you alive is *very* far down on the totem pole. If you've decided that getting your nose reconstructed is your ticket to

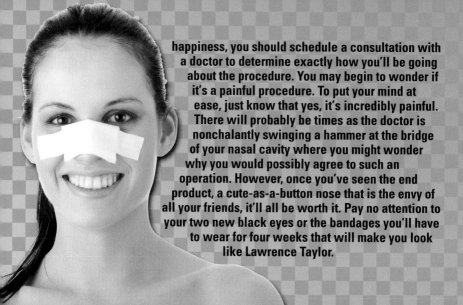

happiness, you should schedule a consultation with a doctor to determine exactly how you'll be going about the procedure. You may begin to wonder if it's a painful procedure. To put your mind at ease, just know that yes, it's incredibly painful. There will probably be times as the doctor is nonchalantly swinging a hammer at the bridge of your nasal cavity where you might wonder why you would possibly agree to such an operation. However, once you've seen the end product, a cute-as-a-button nose that is the envy of all your friends, it'll all be worth it. Pay no attention to your two new black eyes or the bandages you'll have to wear for four weeks that will make you look like Lawrence Taylor.

Lips

Your lips are another area that you may find lacking. If yours are more pencil-thin than a pair of hipster jeans, it may be worth the investment for a richer, fuller experience. To get that Angelina Jolie look (minus the thirty-eight children adopted from sub-Saharan Africa), you just have to make several wise investments in collagen injections or have lip augmentation surgery. This will require either something as simple as a shot or something as complex as a small incision, so it's important to aim for a quality experience. Just remember, if you go with a doctor who doesn't know what he or she is doing, your lips will probably end up looking like four-day-old Jimmy Dean sausages.

Average Cup Size of Female Residents of the Jersey Shore

	1995	2000	2005	2010
D Cup				
C Cup				
B Cup				
A Cup				

The steadily growing confidence in plastic surgery has allowed breast augmentation surgeries to increase exponentially, which has led to measured growth in cup sizes throughout the Shore. While this average may seem high, remember that for every girl with a pair of beestings, there's a chick who thinks size F breasts are becoming.

The chest is an area for many women where bigger is better. While some girls were blessed with mountains for mammaries, others were left with a pair of bee stings and a future job offer as the Secretary General of the Itty Bitty Titty Committee. Unfair plights aside, though, the technology now exists to do something about it. Thanks to an ample dose of silicone and a handful of doctors willing to push the envelope, boobs are getting larger and larger with seemingly no end in sight. At this rate, by the year 2030, some women may be so top-heavy that they'll require complicated series of pulleys and levers just to stay upright (think training wheels but approximately one hundred times more grotesque).

At the Shore, it's no different. The way women seek to get attention from prospective Guidos is through an intricate dance of attraction. OK, it's not very intricate and typically requires only about ten or twelve shots of pure grain alcohol, but it's still a process. That being said, Guido men have historically reacted positively to breasts so big they technically fall under the control of the Bureau of Alcohol, Tobacco, Firearms and Explosives. Consequently, Guidettes rarely see any reason not to go for the gusto with their implants and really raise the bar for what can be considered sexy or in generally good taste. In many ways, this attitude is a natural extension of the Guidette personality, where you look the way you want to look and avoid consideration of how others may feel about it. Even if it means your boobs will inevitably be considered a fire hazard in most public places. When ladies get this procedure, it's important to

focus on a variety of items. First of all, as mentioned above, you should find a size that you're comfortable with and then go a cup size or two bigger. Sure, you will end up accruing a lifetime of back pain and scores of dirty looks from other females, but isn't it a small price to pay to be judged only by one aspect of your body? Plus, the bigger you go, there will be fewer Guidettes in your cup range to contend with. Your second area to consider is how you want your breasts to be shaped. You should definitely go with the "bullet-type" or "miniature basketball" options, since they are the most jarring to look at and can never be found in nature. It will also be more obvious to guys that your boobs are fake, which is important, since straight men spend approximately 53 percent of available brainpower on breasts. **(NOTE: This figure rises to about 98 percent during spring break, when passing mannequins in department stores and during Salma Hayek movies.)**

Finally, if you can opt for some new bolt-ons that are aligned in some sort of

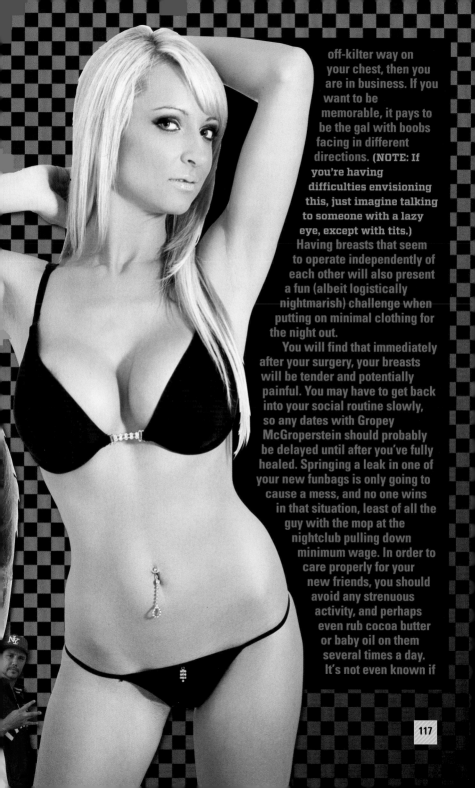

off-kilter way on your chest, then you are in business. If you want to be memorable, it pays to be the gal with boobs facing in different directions. (NOTE: If you're having difficulties envisioning this, just imagine talking to someone with a lazy eye, except with tits.)

Having breasts that seem to operate independently of each other will also present a fun (albeit logistically nightmarish) challenge when putting on minimal clothing for the night out.

You will find that immediately after your surgery, your breasts will be tender and potentially painful. You may have to get back into your social routine slowly, so any dates with Gropey McGroperstein should probably be delayed until after you've fully healed. Springing a leak in one of your new funbags is only going to cause a mess, and no one wins in that situation, least of all the guy with the mop at the nightclub pulling down minimum wage. In order to care properly for your new friends, you should avoid any strenuous activity, and perhaps even rub cocoa butter or baby oil on them several times a day. It's not even known if

117

this will expedite the healing process, but it's totally super hot, and men will respond positively. VERY POSITIVELY.

You will find a great deal of immediate value in your new thoracic investment. You may be gawked at, leered at, whispered about behind your back . . . all the things a young girl dreams of. You may find that your amplifications help open up new doors for you professionally, especially if you work in a gentlemen's club (c'mon Hooters, you know what you are, just accept it). The sheer aggregation of tips could help your boobs achieve a positive return on investment in less than twelve months. **(NOTE: It's actually amazing private equity and venture capital firms haven't keyed in on this niche industry.)** And of course, another side benefit of receiving a breast augmentation is that, in the event of a water landing, your boobs can double as a floatation device. Just remember to affix your mask before assisting others.

Liposuction

Though you will have clearly established a very methodical gym routine by this point, sometimes you need a little extra assistance to iron out some of the trouble spots in your physique. Whether your thighs are as lumpy as instant oatmeal or your stomach has a bigger spare tire than most tractor-trailers, all hope is not lost. You need to recognize the fact that when you hit the gym, you're not just pushing your own limits, but waging a constant battle against your heredity. From time to time, you may just need to give your genetics the kick in the ass they need and invest in some liposuction to shed some of those unwanted pounds quickly and efficiently.

Removing the excess fatty deposits that may dot your exterior may seem like a quick fix and a solution that doesn't address the fundamental root of a problem. That is what makes it so awesome! By accepting the fact that there are some problem areas that you just won't be able to fix, you have given yourself carte blanche to be increasingly lazy, which will most likely manifest itself in a weight-gain-and-loss seesaw (better known by its common name, the Kirstie Alley-go-round). However, this will help you achieve better body image and avoid being photographed for ChubHub.com (again).

The common misconception with liposuction is that it's some sort of overly intrusive procedure that sucks fat out of you using some sort of PVC pipe attached to a

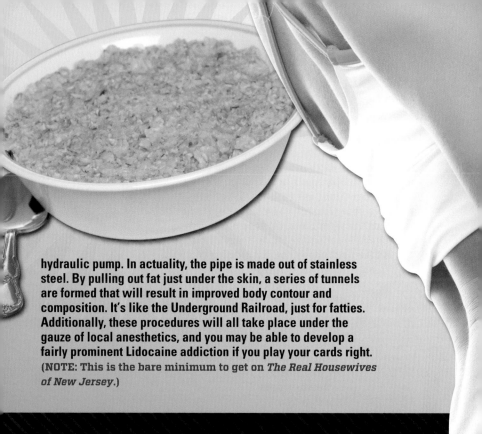

hydraulic pump. In actuality, the pipe is made out of stainless steel. By pulling out fat just under the skin, a series of tunnels are formed that will result in improved body contour and composition. It's like the Underground Railroad, just for fatties. Additionally, these procedures will all take place under the gauze of local anesthetics, and you may be able to develop a fairly prominent Lidocaine addiction if you play your cards right. (NOTE: This is the bare minimum to get on *The Real Housewives of New Jersey*.)

Butt

Guidettes, a killer pair of legs and a great rack are definitely important, but all of these wonderful body parts may be for naught if you have an inferior posterior. Although working out your glutes will generally put you on the fast track to having a bangin' booty, sometimes exercise is not enough. This is all the more pronounced if you have a penchant for eating half a tub of Ben & Jerry's Chubby Hubby before going to bed; let's be honest, some girls have a butt only a professional bowling circuit could love. To remove some of the accrued fat deposits and cellulite around your butt, your doctor will utilize a variety of procedures similar to the steps for liposuction. This will give you all the benefits of a smooth natural taper from buttock to hamstring, as well as allow you to say the words "ass pump" with impunity.

Some of you may not suffer from anything gym-related; instead, you may just have been afflicted with a flat ass since birth. This can be a tragedy, as many otherwise beautiful women have found themselves sadly unable to fill out a pair of Levi's, sometimes even resorting to rolling up athletic socks to simulate a larger ass, a practice commonly derided as butt-lumping. If you are still determined to have a butt like Kim Kardashian, though, all you have to do is be willing to pay for it. The other option you have in this case is to have a close friend perform the operation, which generally involves making incisions at the base of the buttock and inserting makeshift implants fashioned from empty Doritos bags. It probably goes without saying that this will most likely not be covered by your HMO. Butt implants are a generally Butt implants are a generally rare form of surgery at the Jersey

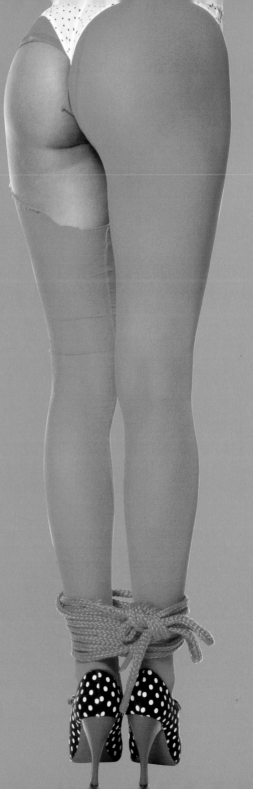

occasionally, these procedures are done to help a gal get that hourglass figure she's always been told by the media she wants (we're looking in your direction, Jessica Rabbit). Once you've decided to go down the path of buttock augmentation, the surgery is fairly straightforward. The doctor will make a small incision in each cheek (unless, of course, you'd prefer to be lopsided) to create a pouch for each saline implant. After the procedure has concluded, you will probably need two to three weeks of rest as you recuperate. This means, ironically, you will drink plenty of fluids and sit on your butt watching television as you heal, activities that would have contributed to making your ass bigger in the first place. In the end, however, you will be able to achieve your desired appearance, as well as to finally start shopping in the Brazilian section at Nordstrom.

You may notice that once you get the ball rolling on artificial enhancement, it can be a slippery slope. But that should be a trait you embrace rather than fear. If God hadn't intended for you to be a 34 EE cup size, then why would he bless an obscure Mexican doctor with the advanced medical knowledge to perform the procedure in the back of a converted hen house? That being said, there may come a time when you want to spread your wings beyond the realm of plastic surgery that is generally considered "safe," "acceptable," or "within the bounds of human decency." Allow us to be your guide.

There aren't a lot of alternative surgeries out there for Guidos, though procedures like calf and penile implants are picking up steam. Strange as it may seem, some guys are so insecure that they think a woman will not be interested in them if their calves are slightly underdeveloped. As a lifeline to these gentlemen with particularly low self-esteem (even for the plastic surgery set), several safe procedures have been developed to provide silicone-based calf implants, albeit at considerable cost. You have to love America. Sure, you could spend several thousand dollars on the seeds of an education, but wouldn't you rather get an elective surgery that will forever stand as a testament to your insecurities? Regarding surgeries around the genital region, let's just say that there are a number of doctors along the Eastern seaboard (some have even helped your local congressman!) who can help you if your—ahem—Italian sausage is not the portion size you had hoped for. These doctors tend to be discreet and comprehensive, and they totally promise never to upload pictures of your pecker on MeSoTiny.com. That's the Hippocratic Oath right there.

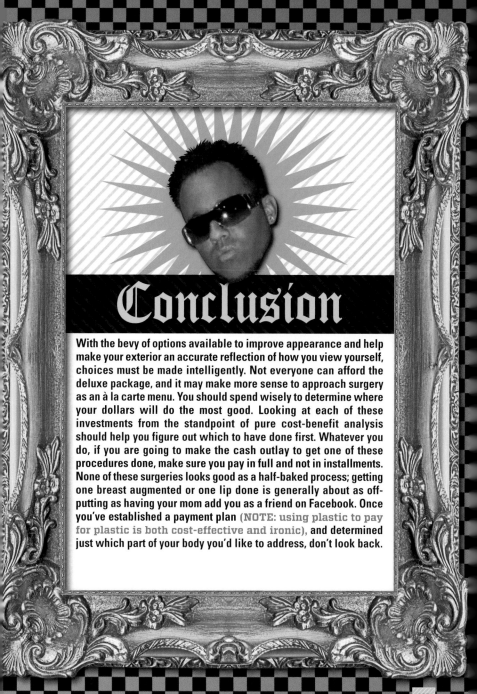

Conclusion

With the bevy of options available to improve appearance and help make your exterior an accurate reflection of how you view yourself, choices must be made intelligently. Not everyone can afford the deluxe package, and it may make more sense to approach surgery as an à la carte menu. You should spend wisely to determine where your dollars will do the most good. Looking at each of these investments from the standpoint of pure cost-benefit analysis should help you figure out which to have done first. Whatever you do, if you are going to make the cash outlay to get one of these procedures done, make sure you pay in full and not in installments. None of these surgeries looks good as a half-baked process; getting one breast augmented or one lip done is generally about as off-putting as having your mom add you as a friend on Facebook. Once you've established a payment plan (NOTE: using plastic to pay for plastic is both cost-effective and ironic), and determined just which part of your body you'd like to address, don't look back.

SMALL SIZE FITS ALL . . . OR, ACCESSORIZING THE GUIDO/GUIDETTE WARDROBE

Looking fresh is such a chief concern that the ideal scenario would essentially be to buy clothes, wear them once, then burn them to preclude repeatability at your favorite night spots. This ensures that you will constantly be painting on a new canvas when meeting the ladies, and all that freed-up space in your closet will allow you to buy that Bowflex you've had your eye on for so long. Beyond being wasteful, though, such a disposable approach to dressing yourself is just impractical from a financial perspective. If you're buying clothes that frequently, then where are you finding your disposable income for gym memberships and ~~steroids~~ vitamin supplements? Regardless, making sure that your wardrobe has the shelf life of a Miley Cyrus song, and that you constantly look good when you go out, demonstrates serious dedication to the GTL creed and should be your ultimate goal.

Tops

For Guidos, the name brand you choose to present to the world is clearly a critical piece of your budding ensemble—Affliction, Christian Audigier, Ed Hardy, Armani Exchange, and the occasional Tapout shirt. All of these brands are core staples of the Guido lifestyle, and venturing into unpopular brands may mean you're scraping the bottom of the barrel when it comes to the potential selection of a mate. Beyond these core brands, however, sometimes you may even see some relic from the Guess outlet store, which is amazing in and of itself, given that no Guess products have been sold since 1989 (coinciding nicely with the fall of the Berlin Wall).

Among the major brands of clothing, Ed Hardy shirts are a particularly popular choice among many members of the Guido set. Inspired originally by tattoos, these shirts are known for their loud colors, fearsome animals, and incredibly high douchebag-per-wear (DPW) ratio. (See highest Douchebaggery per Wear graph on p. 130.) If you are ever unsure whether a shirt is from the Ed Hardy line, just ask yourself if it's something that Helen Keller would design. If so, it probably is, and is ready to be distributed throughout the country at a tremendous markup. It should be noted that these shirts are still awaiting trial at The Hague for crimes against humanity, having caused thousands of people around the world to claw out their

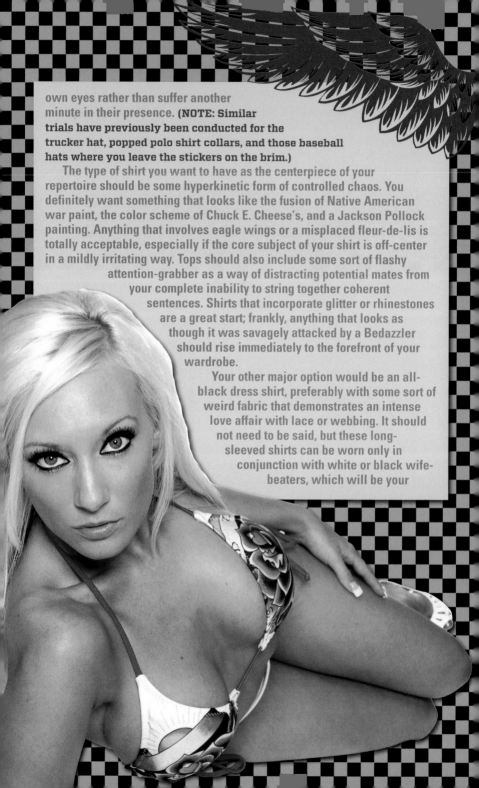

own eyes rather than suffer another minute in their presence. **(NOTE: Similar trials have previously been conducted for the trucker hat, popped polo shirt collars, and those baseball hats where you leave the stickers on the brim.)**

The type of shirt you want to have as the centerpiece of your repertoire should be some hyperkinetic form of controlled chaos. You definitely want something that looks like the fusion of Native American war paint, the color scheme of Chuck E. Cheese's, and a Jackson Pollock painting. Anything that involves eagle wings or a misplaced fleur-de-lis is totally acceptable, especially if the core subject of your shirt is off-center in a mildly irritating way. Tops should also include some sort of flashy attention-grabber as a way of distracting potential mates from your complete inability to string together coherent sentences. Shirts that incorporate glitter or rhinestones are a great start; frankly, anything that looks as though it was savagely attacked by a Bedazzler should rise immediately to the forefront of your wardrobe.

Your other major option would be an all-black dress shirt, preferably with some sort of weird fabric that demonstrates an intense love affair with lace or webbing. It should not need to be said, but these long-sleeved shirts can be worn only in conjunction with white or black wife-beaters, which will be your

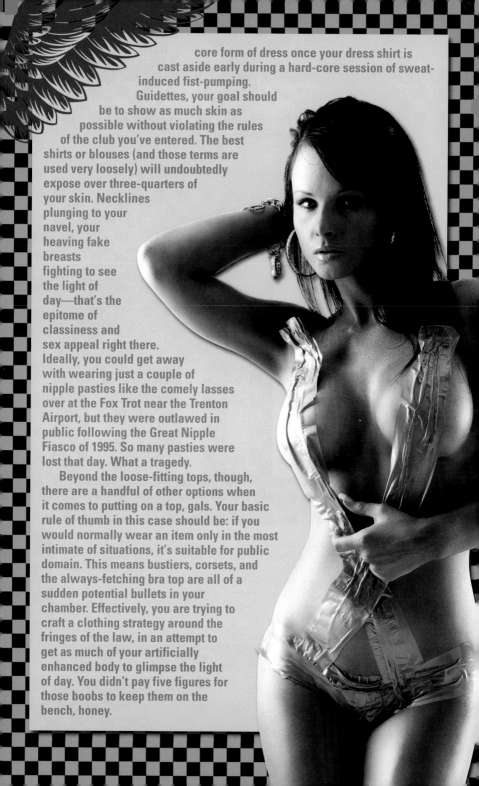

core form of dress once your dress shirt is cast aside early during a hard-core session of sweat-induced fist-pumping.

Guidettes, your goal should be to show as much skin as possible without violating the rules of the club you've entered. The best shirts or blouses (and those terms are used very loosely) will undoubtedly expose over three-quarters of your skin. Necklines plunging to your navel, your heaving fake breasts fighting to see the light of day—that's the epitome of classiness and sex appeal right there. Ideally, you could get away with wearing just a couple of nipple pasties like the comely lasses over at the Fox Trot near the Trenton Airport, but they were outlawed in public following the Great Nipple Fiasco of 1995. So many pasties were lost that day. What a tragedy.

Beyond the loose-fitting tops, though, there are a handful of other options when it comes to putting on a top, gals. Your basic rule of thumb in this case should be: if you would normally wear an item only in the most intimate of situations, it's suitable for public domain. This means bustiers, corsets, and the always-fetching bra top are all of a sudden potential bullets in your chamber. Effectively, you are trying to craft a clothing strategy around the fringes of the law, in an attempt to get as much of your artificially enhanced body to glimpse the light of day. You didn't pay five figures for those boobs to keep them on the bench, honey.

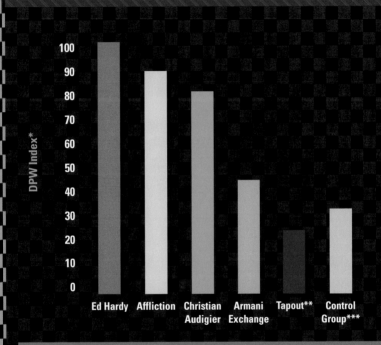

Highest Douchebaggery per Wear (DPW)

DPW Index*

100	
90	
80	
70	
60	
50	
40	
30	
20	
10	
0	

Ed Hardy · Affliction · Christian Audigier · Armani Exchange · Tapout** · Control Group***

*The relative partying index (RPI) is calibrated as follows: a score of 0 equates to a plain shirt that cost less than $5 while a score of 100 is equal to what an investment banker on Wall Street would wear the day after getting his annual bonus.

**Participants who wear Tapout tend to be more overt meatheads as opposed to pure douchebags. Besides, we and the editors are at least slightly afraid of them. Let's just move on.

***The control group consists of all other existing brand's, such as Banana Republic, Gap, J.Crew, Abercrombie & Fitch, and four-year-old Mervyn's hand-me-downs.

CHRISTIAN AUDIGIER:

In an effort to distinguish themselves from Ed Hardy without actually distinguishing anything, Christian Audigier spun off. An excellent choice for any Guido looking for pretend uniqueness.

ED HARDY:

The gold standard for male Guido wear, Ed Hardy shirts are notable for their bright colors, exotic animals, and the shiny materials they have been fashioned from.

AFFLICTION:

Stemming from an origin in MMA (mixed martial arts), Affliction came on the scene to outclass the Tapout craze. Nothing says "tough guy" like shiny, swirling designs and rhinestone dragons. A Guido must.

ARMANI EXCHANGE:

No wardrobe is complete without an excessive volume of A/X clothing. You can spill beer on five A/X shirts for the price of one Armani shirt, and let's face it, your Taco Tuesday shirt is not in good shape after Margarita Monday.

TAPOUT:

Rocking some solid Tapout gear will basically let everyone around you know that at the drop of a hat, you may snap and start kicking ass like Patrick Swayze in *Road House*. There might not be a lot of variation among this brand, but when you're as menacing as a pair of brass knuckles, who's going to tell you you're unoriginal?

When it comes to going out, Guidos should try to wear varieties of upscale jeans that accentuate the general genital region as well as both butt cheeks. (NOTE: Only one would be rather off-putting.) This means getting well acquainted with brands like True Religion (though no one has ever looked good in these, unless they are as lumpy as mashed potatoes) and Seven. These manufacturers are good at making each new pair of jeans that roll off their assembly lines look like it has been on a construction site for two years. Each premade rip, tear, distressed mark, and hole will be like an aphrodisiac to the lucky ladies you encounter. Jeans that go the extra mile and incorporate bleach and/or dirt are also highly prized, as every woman wants to find a man who displays no clear understanding of how to properly clean or dress himself.

The jeans that Guidettes wear are an incredibly personal reflection of the styles you like, the subtle cat-and-mouse game of what you'd like to reveal and what you'd

like to keep hidden, and a tacit understanding that guys always want to be kept guessing. Just kidding. Much like the tops you wear, when it comes to jeans, you should typically opt for the ones with holes so large they appear to have suffered a run-in with an Iowa grain thresher. Denim is a fairly coarse material after all, so the less of it that touches your skin, the more comfortable you will inevitably be. And let's be honest, once you meet that Guido of your dreams, those jeans will end up slung over a bedpost in a highly accusatory fashion anyway. Just remember, less is more.

For some occasions, it may make more sense for the Guidettes to select a pair of booty shorts to hit the town with. The appropriate length of these shorts is open to debate. While some Rhodes scholars argue that there should be some sense of decorum, advocating a chaste covering of the labia and related lady parts, others have mentioned that Brody Jenner's ascendance as a generational voice has thrown all modesty and restraint out the window. To that end, we must advise the reader: just go with whatever feels natural. You should certainly aim for a pair of shorts tight enough to accomplish two ends: constricting proper blood flow and providing a nice canvas for your muffin-top. How short you decide to go is really just a matter of personal pride and self-respect. (NOTE: May not apply.)

Footwear

Guidos will generally wear shoes that are as fresh as possible, with nary a smudge to be seen. The slightest violation of your shoes is a serious matter that should be rectified immediately, via saliva or hydrogen peroxide. Puma, Nike, Reebok, and Adidas are all highly popular, as long as what you're purchasing is a shade of white that blinds anyone within direct line of sight. In terms of dress shoes, anything Italian-sounding from the DSW or the closest outlet store will suffice, especially if they are as shiny as your face after a three-hour dance marathon.

There are obviously a myriad of footwear options for women, though it's generally

fairly easy to choose something appropriate. Thigh-high boots that would make a female superhero blush are an acceptable choice that is appropriate for an astonishing array of occasions. Heels are also vital parts of the Guidette lifestyle. It's amazing that most four-inch heels can have such a profound effect on your height, just as they radically alter your balance so much you may think you have some sort of inner-ear infection. These types of shoe products can be viewed as interchangeable, and you will amaze yourself at the variety of applications and events you can wear them to. This means thigh-highs and heels can penetrate locales that may not immediately seem appropriate, like church, the orthodontist, or relay races.

Accessories

SUNGLASSES The selection of sunglasses is a critical decision for most Guidos. Ideally, you want to hone in on a pair that costs approximately one to two months' rent, so you will be that much more apocalyptically angry when you lose them, sit on them, or break them during one of your frequent street tussles. Name brands are obviously vitally important for accessories like sunglasses, and you should try to select a pair that is polarized to a degree where none of the girls can see where you're looking. Glasses that are diamond- or ruby-encrusted are generally the most popular on the shore, though topaz-encrusted models may be leading the next charge. It's always better to be an early adopter.

As for the Guidettes, ideally you want to wear glasses that cover approximately 82 percent of your face. Your chin should be the only thing exposed to the sun's harmful rays, and even that is negotiable. Basically, you are looking for a facial coverage strategy similar to one of those 1940s fighter pilots with the enormous goggles or Kareem Abdul-Jabbar late in his NBA career; either is acceptable. Effectively, any pair that covers your face roughly the same as two coffee saucers is the bare minimum you should find acceptable.

HEADWEAR In terms of headwear, the Shore is not as varied as your typical haberdashery. Most Guidos and Guidettes are extremely wary of disturbing a hairdo they have spent three or four hours crafting. Occasionally, you will see headbands make an appearance at the clubs, mainly from the younger set. In many ways, this is a smart maneuver for a young man who has demonstrated difficulties maintaining his own blowout, and the headband will provide the optical illusion that his hair crests higher than it does in actuality. This is also the only place in the Western hemisphere where you will see white guys wearing Kangol hats. Most other locales have realized that that is just a recipe to get Samuel L. Jackson over there and kicking ass in a moment's notice.

NECKLACES Necklaces are a great way for you to express yourself, especially if you think the best way to introduce yourself to new people is through the gauze of five pounds of fake gold you purchased from a vending machine at the Stop & Shop. A necklace is also another great place for an intricate cross, in case anyone who has not seen your preponderance of religious or tribal tattoos still has some sort of question regarding your belief system. Girls are also expected to wear a ridiculous amount of necklaces, bracelets, rings, and other baubles, so as to temporarily confuse and intrigue potential mates.

The sexes demonstrate distinct differences when it comes to earrings. Guidos should generally opt for diamond studs—the bigger the better. If you can get some sort of spinner installed like the rims on a rapper's Escalade, that's even better. Your goal should be to be gaudy and ridiculous, and if you can't find something that makes enough of a spectacle of yourself, don't hesitate to save your wallet and go cubic zirconia. Most Guidettes you'll be meeting on the boardwalk are not CIA-certified jewelers. Guidettes will typically opt for hoop earrings with a wide enough diameter to qualify them as hula hoops in most locales. The rule here is fairly simple: the more ostentatious, the better.

Hygiene Basics

For Guidos, smelling good is a great way to accentuate all the hard work and effort that you put into your body. While some segments of society recommend a subtle or soft-pedaled approach to cologne and deodorant, what is the point of giving yourself some assistance in the smell department if it can be detected only within a very narrow window? You

· INTRODUCING ·

JUICED

COLOGNE *for* GUIDOS

should realistically be noticeable at twenty paces, perhaps even thirty. This means taking a shower in your scent du jour as though you were bathing in tomato sauce after being sprayed by a skunk. The two situations are closer relatives than you might think at first glance.

From a cologne perspective, you definitely want to focus on fragrances that haven't been popular for over a decade. Cool Water is a great example. If you're like every asshole who wears the newest concoction from Kenneth Cole, it will be hard to differentiate you from the sprawling mass of humanity within the club. But if you're the guy rocking a scent from the halcyon days of the Clinton Administration, that may transport your potential hook up back to fonder memories, reminding her of joyous prosperity and a simpler time. Oh, and you'll probably get laid.

As for deodorant, you should opt for one of the many body-spray-type deodorants on the market today, which provide the dual function of (a) an additional overpowering smell by which to flummox the ladies and; (b) a cursory attempt to actually deodorize your armpits, which all but guarantees you will smell like a curious mixture of hot garbage within two or three hours. Regardless of whether you smell like roses or a smattering of fecal matter, the eighteen or nineteen drinks all bar and club attendees will imbibe throughout the course of the night should render most olfactory senses useless, so all of your preparations in this area may be futile.

Maintaining Your Wardrobe

It's not only about buying the latest and greatest fashions, though. You have to demonstrate a clear and unimpeachable willingness to keep your clothes constantly clean. This means either having a top-end washer-and-dryer combination on your premises, or at least having a laundromat within a stone's throw of where you live. (NOTE: Having a laundromat next to your gym or tanning salon can help you save time that can be reallocated into stomach crunches.)

Ideally, you should wash every article after each incidence of wear, given your mandate to maintain as fresh an appearance as possible. Even better would be to wash every item by itself to ensure cleanliness and avoid color leaching. In order to avoid color cross-pollination during the washing process, it is also recommended that you employ a targeted strategy for washing your clothes as well. While "whites" and "colors" may work well for some, it's best to play it safe and wash each color only with congruent shades to avoid any potential calamity. This means having a niche sorting process, incorporating groups like "eggshell white," "forest green," and "cerulean." The only way you'll avoid those potentially embarrassing missteps and be forced to start from scratch is to maintain a strict adherence to color segregation, which will also make you seem super OCD at the laundromat, and people will probably keep a safe distance.

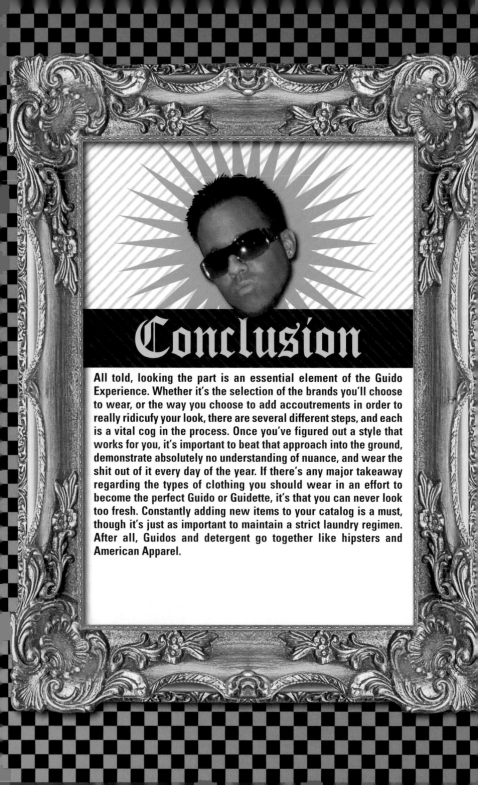

Conclusion

All told, looking the part is an essential element of the Guido Experience. Whether it's the selection of the brands you'll choose to wear, or the way you choose to add accoutrements in order to really ridicufy your look, there are several different steps, and each is a vital cog in the process. Once you've figured out a style that works for you, it's important to beat that approach into the ground, demonstrate absolutely no understanding of nuance, and wear the shit out of it every day of the year. If there's any major takeaway regarding the types of clothing you should wear in an effort to become the perfect Guido or Guidette, it's that you can never look too fresh. Constantly adding new items to your catalog is a must, though it's just as important to maintain a strict laundry regimen. After all, Guidos and detergent go together like hipsters and American Apparel.

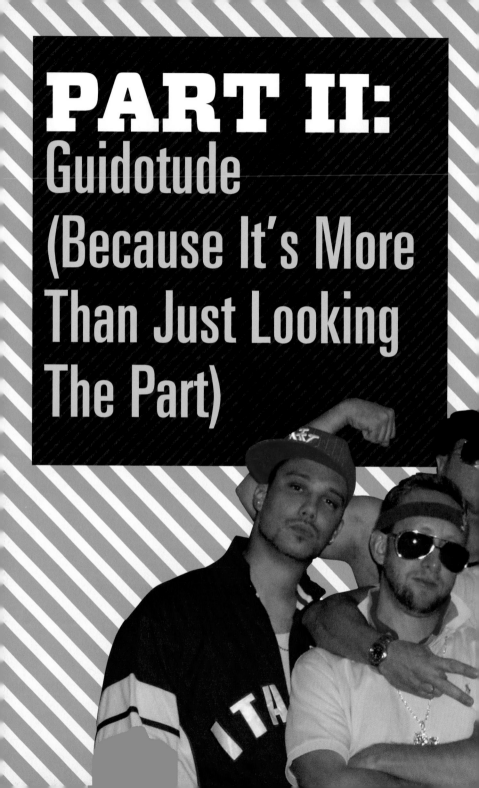

PART II:
Guidotude
(Because It's More Than Just Looking The Part)

GET A PERSONALITY (AND TRY TO AVOID A TRIP TO THE SPANK BANK)

Having the body of Adonis, a sick tan, and the best clothes will all be moot if you can't provide the swagger to match your exterior. This means that you have to bring your A-game when it comes to developing the right attitude, knowing what to say and when to say it, and how to respond in the face of immediate boardwalk danger. Beyond just being able to handle yourself, your style and outlook should be clear to everyone who meets you, either from a simple interaction or from a photo circulating the Internet of you and eight of your dickbag friends. Once you've figured out how to cultivate the right mindset, you will find yourself at the epicenter of the Guido Universe (and no, we're not referring to Tony's Pizza Shack in Wildwood). To really demonstrate your inner confidence, we recommend several facets of your personality to concentrate on improving, as well as several actions that can produce incredible results.

Speech

It is when you are conversing with other males of the species *Guidus sapiens* that the crucial alpha-male hierarchy is determined. Beyond just physical altercations, it is important to constantly challenge other potential alpha males via the spoken word. This is primarily achieved through "big-leaguing." By this, we are referring to little needling ways to subtly disrespect someone, by not actually referring to them by name. Examples include "bro," "chief," "tiger," "pal," and "buddy." These sorts of words are crucial parts of your vocabulary, and are extremely vital when you have nothing else of value to say. **(NOTE: This could be a fairly common phenomenon, so pay attention.)**

The word "bro" has rightfully assumed its important place in the dialect of Jerseyites for generations. For historical reference, the current record for bros per hour (BPH) was set by Mario Ligonace of Parnassus, New Jersey, during a particularly contentious Fourth of July dispute in 1993. During several points in a long and winding diatribe that somehow managed to encompass the failure of the Yankees to secure a productive left-fielder at the trading deadline, as well as his continued irritation with the quality of recent batches of Mama DiGiorno's garlic meat sauce, Mr. Ligonace uttered the word so frequently and with such a staccato delivery that those surrounding him believed he was speaking in tongues and having a religious experience. Mr. Ligonace managed to utter the word "bro" 216 times in thirteen minutes of uninterrupted rant, equating to a BPH of 997, which has in recent years been approached only during Italian Pride Day parades. History buffs can see a bronzed statue of Mr. Ligonace performing his famed rant on the boardwalk in Belmar, between the cotton candy stand and the store that sells offensive t-shirts.

Something about New Jersey makes utterance of the word "bro" far more likely; it's as though passing through the turnpike automatically triggers some sort of endorphin release in your brain. Though other states have tried to keep up with a variety of Bro Enhancement

145

Bro Pie Graph

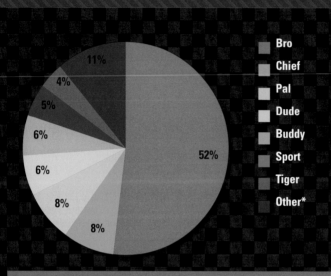

- Bro
- Chief
- Pal
- Dude
- Buddy
- Sport
- Tiger
- Other*

52%
11%
4%
5%
6%
6%
8%
8%

*"Other" include articles like fella, dude-a-rino, fucktard, chieftain, broham, brohamlet, broham-and-cheese, and guy.

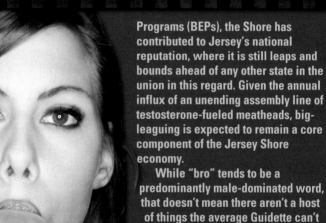

Programs (BEPs), the Shore has contributed to Jersey's national reputation, where it is still leaps and bounds ahead of any other state in the union in this regard. Given the annual influx of an unending assembly line of testosterone-fueled meatheads, big-leaguing is expected to remain a core component of the Jersey Shore economy.

While "bro" tends to be a predominantly male-dominated word, that doesn't mean there aren't a host of things the average Guidette can't learn regarding how to speak properly. **(NOTE: Suck on that triple negative, MLA handbook!)** It is required under the Guidette Bill of

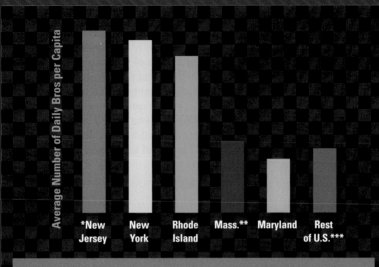

Top States for Bros per Capita, Daily Average

Average Number of Daily Bros per Capita

*New Jersey · New York · Rhode Island · Mass.** · Maryland · Rest of U.S.***

*New Jersey holds a dominating position in this landscape, hence its title as the "Center of the Bro-niverse."
**Unfortunately, nearly 75 percent of the bros uttered in this state are directly related to cheering on the Red Sox or Patriots, which makes these folks incredibly fucking insufferable.
***Average number of bros said per day by the rest of the nation, meager at best.

Rights (Article 3 for those scoring at home) that all girls you don't know or have not seen before be referred to uniformly as "skanks." This rule is applied regardless of their sexual appetite and history, whether or not those facts are even known to you. The goal in this case is to remove any and all credibility from women you don't know and to stoke the flames of a vicious catfight at all times.

It is also important to remember that speech isn't just what you say, but how you say it. It is recommended that you chew gum constantly (and by chew gum, we mean smack it audibly enough that it will be distracting to people on adjacent streets), as that will give you the air of someone who doesn't care what other people think. This is truly important for your ultimate goal: the hard-hearted girl with the tough exterior who gets swept up by her Prince Charming. It's like a rom com with Sandra Bullock and Hugh Grant, except that (a) you won't want to shoot yourself in the head afterward, and (b) your Prince Charming will definitely have a tan and know his way around a weight room.

Attitude

Developing a meaningful swagger is a vital part of the Guido experience. While we have already covered the importance of your words, sometimes you can convey just as much about your personality without uttering a single "bro." It's recommended you develop nonverbal methods of communication like raising your eyebrows to express surprise, or leaving your mouth agape to convey astonishment that you gave your girlfriend herpes (she probably got it from the hot tub). Additionally, learn to speak with your hands to punctuate important points of emphasis. (NOTE: We could have brought up the old tired joke about how an Italian speech impediment is when one arm is longer than the other, but we're better than that.)

As far as your overall attitude goes, it's important to develop your self-esteem to the point where you can't ever fathom yourself being wrong. This sort of bullheadedness is critical within the Guido community, as it will undoubtedly assist you in participating in dozens of pointless fights, as well as make you incapable of engaging in any sort of serious long-term relationship. By relying only on yourself, you will also ensure that you never have to do any stupid shit like gain insight from a trusted colleague or become exposed to a new point of view. In order to foster the appropriate attitude and chutzpah to live the Guido lifestyle, you should just pretend that you live in a consequence-free environment, where nothing you do or say could possibly have any negative outcomes.

Responding to Perceived Slights

Despite your generally docile manner, there will be instances where actions will speak louder than words. Occasionally you will run into the rare (OK, not so rare) Guido who is just itching for a fight, and confrontation will be inevitable. This is the type of guy who talks so much shit that the sheer volume of excrement he emits into the atmosphere would get his house listed as a Superfund site, and his movements would be monitored constantly by the EPA. Sadly, this sort of adversary is a frequent visitor to the Shore and always tends to overstay his welcome, but there are clear ways to deal with such a regrettable situation.

In order to defend yourself against an aggressor's accusations of your "punkness," it's important to respond forcefully, usually with the well-thought-out, clever emotional maturity that goes into the average YouTube comment. This means finding your opponent's verbal pressure points and badgering him until both of you have your fists cocked, locked, and ready to rock. What follows is a graceful ballet of insults, male posturing, and inappropriate gestures. You should focus on a particular weak spot of your opponent's outward appearance—a bald spot, lack of upper body, perhaps even a molester mustache. From that point on, you should focus all of your slights in that vein, but take great care in maintaining a running conversation with him, peppered with plenty of "bros" and "pals." This allows you to maintain the air of trying to play the role of peacemaker, when clearly you're trying to knock this guy into next week. Adding crotch grabs or spitting repeatedly is also a nice touch, in that it will probably make you seem at least borderline insane or at least devoid of boundaries. This sort of meandering dialogue and pantomime will also be humorous to boardwalk traffic, and will be especially endearing when a video of the event inevitably surfaces on the Internet.

When you're actually fighting, it's important to go for knockout blows with every swing of your fist. If you're not trying to end this thing in one shot, then the longer this ordeal drags on, the greater the likelihood that your $80 Armani Exchange white t-shirt will get an unruly bloodstain on it. If this is what you're aiming for, you should start busting out wildly inaccurate uppercuts like Don Flamenco from *Mike Tyson's Punch-Out!!* (NOTE: We have a new leader in the clubhouse for obscure analogies) on the off chance that one manages to connect. If you catch your enemy flush on the chin, odds are he'll crumple to his knees immediately, much like the women you will inevitably meet at a later point this evening. If this one-punch strategy proves difficult, you can also opt for chokeholds, arm bars, or a well-placed stomach punch to subdue your future victim. At NO POINT are shots to the groin acceptable, given that this isn't a Home Alone movie. When the dust has settled and the major points of dissension have been resolved (e.g., your fist was not previously as well versed with his teeth), the aftermath will typically proceed in one of two ways. Either the two of you will collect yourselves and slink off respectfully like gladiators of yore, or the cops will get involved and one of you will be trying to cauterize a bloody nose and give a police report simultaneously.

Perhaps the most important vessel for your newfound attitude to make itself known is through the taking of ludicrous photos to document your evenings out about town. It's vital to chronicle these moments, as the combination of undistilled alcohol and highly concentrated energy drinks will probably make you black out before you've ever set foot out the door. It's not simply a matter of looking straight ahead and trying to look candid; these pictures will soon be on Facebook, and if you don't pose appropriately, you'll have to spend your days untagging photos when you could be looking for a job instead.

A key component of taking a good photo is how you convey your attitude by the way you look. If you Guidos want to look tough, you definitely should pucker your lips and tilt your head slightly upward. Onlookers will assume that either you are a real hard-ass, or you are just practicing your fellatio techniques for after-hours activities. If you can make sure to incorporate as much lip gloss as possible (c'mon, it's metrosexual!) you will definitely be the shining beacon the camera latches onto. It's not all about adopting a vacant stare and looking menacing, though; other factors are just as essential. You should make sure that your bronzer is applied as evenly as possible; otherwise your skin will end up having more shades than a Benetton ad. Another requirement when you decide to take a photo is that all your friends must be in the picture with you at the same time, and everyone must look the same. This congruency not only will be mildly creepy, but also may finally get people talking about the ethical ramifications of cloning. Once you are all assembled and look like an army of the eminently unemployable, it's time to add the icing on the cake. To show just how much of a bad-ass you are, you should throw up your forefinger and your middle finger in front of you like you're making the number two, or you're pretending to be a Japanese girl between the ages of thirteen and twenty-eight.

Just as the guys have a checklist when it comes to taking pictures, every Guidette should know what she's doing when it comes to being in a snapshot. The goal in this case is fairly simple: you gals should attempt to look as slutty as possible without exposing enough of your areolas to get you sent to county jail. Now that's not simply a matter of clothing—there are plenty of ways to give off a slutty demeanor without dressing too provocatively (though tragically, *Girls Gone Wild: Bringum Young University* still remains the worst-selling installment of the franchise). This is all too often borne out by photographic evidence. Between scripted girl-on-girl make-out sessions, women pushing their boobs together, and girls lifting their skirts to show a curious disdain for undergarments . . . well, frankly, it's all awesome. In order to be a true Guidette, you have to show an unwavering desire to own your sexuality, so what

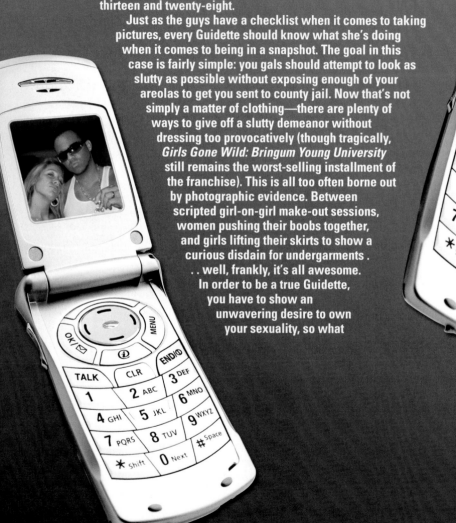

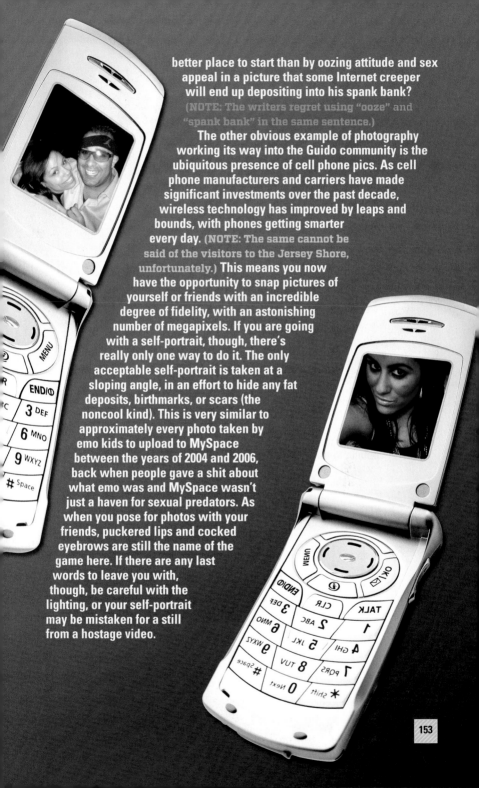

better place to start than by oozing attitude and sex appeal in a picture that some Internet creeper will end up depositing into his spank bank? (NOTE: The writers regret using "ooze" and "spank bank" in the same sentence.)

The other obvious example of photography working its way into the Guido community is the ubiquitous presence of cell phone pics. As cell phone manufacturers and carriers have made significant investments over the past decade, wireless technology has improved by leaps and bounds, with phones getting smarter every day. (NOTE: The same cannot be said of the visitors to the Jersey Shore, unfortunately.) This means you now have the opportunity to snap pictures of yourself or friends with an incredible degree of fidelity, with an astonishing number of megapixels. If you are going with a self-portrait, though, there's really only one way to do it. The only acceptable self-portrait is taken at a sloping angle, in an effort to hide any fat deposits, birthmarks, or scars (the noncool kind). This is very similar to approximately every photo taken by emo kids to upload to MySpace between the years of 2004 and 2006, back when people gave a shit about what emo was and MySpace wasn't just a haven for sexual predators. As when you pose for photos with your friends, puckered lips and cocked eyebrows are still the name of the game here. If there are any last words to leave you with, though, be careful with the lighting, or your self-portrait may be mistaken for a still from a hostage video.

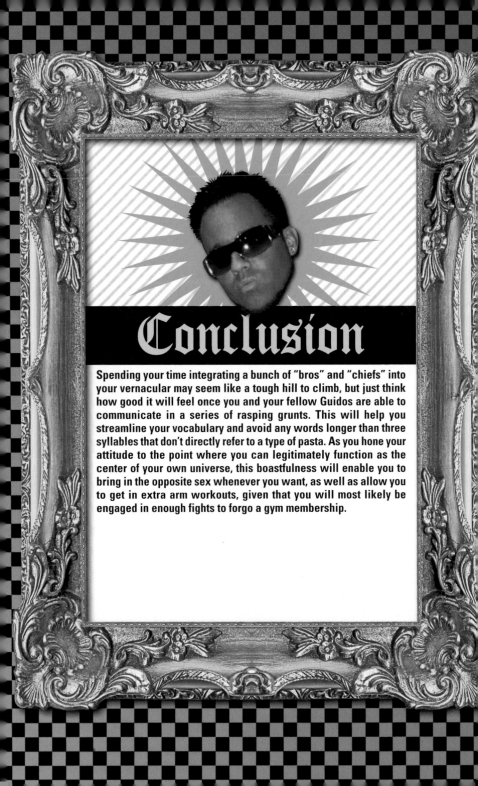

Conclusion

Spending your time integrating a bunch of "bros" and "chiefs" into your vernacular may seem like a tough hill to climb, but just think how good it will feel once you and your fellow Guidos are able to communicate in a series of rasping grunts. This will help you streamline your vocabulary and avoid any words longer than three syllables that don't directly refer to a type of pasta. As you hone your attitude to the point where you can legitimately function as the center of your own universe, this boastfulness will enable you to bring in the opposite sex whenever you want, as well as allow you to get in extra arm workouts, given that you will most likely be engaged in enough fights to forgo a gym membership.

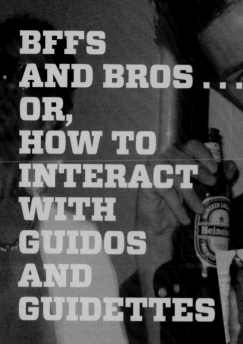

BFFS AND BROS . . . OR, HOW TO INTERACT WITH GUIDOS AND GUIDETTES

It's been said before that no man is an island. Trying to go it alone, in any part of your life, can be a recipe for disaster. Without developing solid, long-lasting friendships, you can miss out on many of the best parts of life: you and your friends renting a couple of speedboats and determining whether you can safely navigate a vessel while simultaneously fist-pumping; finding a best man for your wedding to that girl who works at the nail salon over in Spring Lake; you and the girls going out to a club and getting thrown out for fighting (OK, this will probably happen too many times to count). All of this joyous potential is even more apparent once you hit the boardwalk. As soon as you set foot on those creaky planks (adroitly dodging the used condoms and crushed cans of Monster Energy), you will soon find yourself in a world where you've got to constantly keep your head on a swivel. So, finding a Guido or Guidette who will have your back and help you sail through these potentially turbulent waters is imperative. At the very least, idiocy loves company.

Male Bonding

The bond between Guidos can run deep. Finding a best friend can mean finding a confidant and associate for every aspect of your life. This means having someone to spot you while you're at the gym, a bro to help ensure that you've received an appropriately even tan, and a buddy that can even let you know whether the Ed Hardy shirt you're wearing tonight clashes with your shiny jeans. (NOTE: The quick answer is yes, it does.) The point is, it's vital to have someone who will shoot you straight, albeit with the hard-hitting, well-constructed insight of a Dan Brown novel.

There comes a time in many Guido bromances when jealousy can rear its ugly head. It's only natural; the Shore's combination of dramatic levels of testosterone and scantily clad (if clad at all) women creates a potentially combustible cocktail when it comes to friendships. There will be times when you and a close friend end up lusting after the same girl. While in other parts of society a pervasive attitude of "bros before hoes" would take root, strange things can happen under the siren's spell that is $8 handles of vodka. When you and your buddy are both in hot pursuit of the same lucky lady, some clearly defined rules of engagement apply.

If you find that your buddy has a good thing going with a particular lady friend, it is generally good manners not to try to have sex with her. That's just common courtesy. You will notice that even if you are blatantly hitting on your friend's girlfriend and she rebuffs your disgustingly explicit advances, your friend will blame her regardless. This is because it is a time-honored tenet of the Guido code that guys will never immediately blame other guys within the community, because it is expected that there will be times when your lecherous behavior will be out of your control. If you can avoid precipitating any potential confrontation with a good buddy, you've just decreased by 80 percent your chances of having a workout partner drop a weightlifting bar on your trachea during a bench press. Trust the math.

Female Bonding

The deep friendships a female forms are a critical part of growing up, or at least that seems to be the main take away from *The Sisterhood of the Traveling Pants*. Similarly, the characters in *Sex and the City* showed that a woman is defined by more than whom she's dating or what she does for a living (these were the two or three minutes of the show when Samantha wasn't fucking some guy). At the Jersey Shore, these friendships demonstrate a high frequency of parallels, albeit with additional bronzer and more cleavage.

True Guidette friendships play an important role in social dynamics, especially when going out at night. You ideally want to find a crew of girls to drink with back at the house, and then unleash your collective fury at the variety of nightclubs foolish enough to stand in your path. In many cases,

women will embrace their roles as sexual paramours and give themselves racy nicknames that would in any other context be unflattering—something along the lines of "The Tramp Troop," "The Skank Bank," or "The Whore Corps." It's important to let potential mates know right where they'll stand with you and your group and exactly what you are looking for. Men are generally too stupid to pick up on any form of subtle cues, even if you are dressed in clothes that weigh less than a contact lens.

Unfortunately, there are many instances that expose the bonds between women as tenuous at best. The penchant among this gender for backstabbing, man-stealing, and general bitchy behavior is actually quite impressive, and is pretty much the only reason the Lifetime network still exists today. The source of most of these problems is obviously the introduction of men into the equation, as oftentimes women will butt heads over the same Guido. (NOTE: Ironically, his goal 95 percent of the time under those circumstances will be a threesome.) If there's any takeaway for the ladies in this situation, it's that there will always be another Guido. Don't wreck a potentially beautiful friendship over a man. Even if it may seem that you'd be happier with that juicehead in your life, the grass is always greener on the other side, and the Ed Hardy shirt on the other side always has more skulls.

Performing Your Duties as Wingman or Wingwoman

There comes the time in every male friendship when you'll need to assist a friend who has established a strong rapport with a particularly fetching member of the opposite sex. In many cases, this may mean that you will have to sacrifice your usual standards and keep the girl's friend busy. Every once in a while, this will result in your having the opportunity to hook up with a beautiful woman who has no choice but to focus on you since her friend is otherwise occupied. However, that is the exception, not the rule. Far more frequently, you will be put in the position of dealing with more threes and fours than a Soviet judge during Olympic

the bullet, swallow your pride, and pray for some applied short-term memory loss. At the very least, you can take solace in the fact that these things tend to follow a karmic balance, so that any good deed you perform for your friend will be repaid to you fivefold. That means he'll have to hook up with a chick five times as fat. And that's ammunition for the rest of your lives.

Once you've managed to wrap your head around such an insidious equation, you actually have to "jump" on the grenade. The gory details will be spared in this case, but you can probably imagine what this entails. Let's just say there is at least a 50 percent chance you may develop some sort of post-traumatic stress disorder, and the mere sight of a heifer may forever cause you to weep violently. The next morning, as you shake off the vestiges of yet another hangover, you may catch a glimpse of the manatee you speared the night before. While this may provide the same look of horror and bewilderment on your face as the first time you watched "Two Girls, One Cup," soon after you will be awash in the feeling of a good deed done. Then you will probably find your friend and threaten his life, perhaps even with some sort of blunt object. That's what friends are for.

Guidettes, let's be frank: the number of times you will need to fulfill a role as wingwoman is very limited. It's not too often you'll find a situation where a Guidette will get picked up by some juicehead at a bar, but his friend won't let him go home with her. In fact, it's probably safe to say that such a scenario has

gymnastics. This is a delicate process known as "jumping on the grenade," with which you surely have a nodding acquaintance (and may be a role you have performed a handful of times).

Jumping on the grenade is one of the wingman's major duties, perhaps the most important task he will be assigned in the course of a night's events. A true wingman never complains about the unfortunate set of circumstances that may lead him to the bed of a woman who doesn't exactly appeal to him. The correct response to such a harrowing state of affairs is to bite

TELLING TIME WASTED

2 A.M.

2 P.M.

played out exactly zero times in the history of ever. There will be times, however, when one of your gal pals has her eyes on a particularly fetching Guido, and it will be your job to subtly seduce a friend of his to make sure that her train to Unplanned Pregnancyville won't get derailed. If you see one of your friends starting to make nice with a fella, but he's got a buddy lurking in the background, do your friend a favor and flirt with the other guy a little. The worst-case scenario is you'll probably get him to buy you a couple of cheap well drinks and maybe have a sloppy public make-out session. OK, actually, the worst-case scenario is he gets your number and stalks you for eight months. But even then, you can change your number and begin the cycle anew.

WHAT'S THE CUP FOR?

Friend in the Rotation

Though it's sad to say, sometimes in this society, people are judged unfairly because of their looks. Clearly, this must be a shocking revelation to you, so we understand if you need to sit down for a moment to collect your thoughts. Just as pretty people in America are offered boundless opportunities, you'll find that most people shoveling shit don't exactly look like Brad Pitt or Jessica Alba. Despite this glaring inequity, there's a way to make it work for you. Every Guidette posse needs to have at least one girl who doesn't fit in with the rest of the crew and makes every other girl look significantly better by comparison. This will allow you to feel like you're performing an act of charity by being so inclusive, which is important because on most of your nights out, you'll be engaging primarily in shallow, selfish behavior.

   When you're on the lookout for an ugly future friend, you want to make sure that she's not too jaw-droppingly ugly. After all, you'll be in this

wildebeest's presence in order to reap the benefit of being "contrastually attractive" (or "contrasctive," if you will), not to be completely run out of a photograph by her fugly. If she's particularly unattractive, it's inevitable that a photo will start circulating the Internet faster than a well-placed Rickroll, but none of the eyeballs will be looking in your direction. You should be searching for a girl who: (a) likes to party; (b) is either too tall or too short; (c) is slightly heavyset; and/or (d) constantly talks about how badly she needs to get laid. Bonus points if she drinks herself into oblivion every time you go out, and is unafraid to get out on the dance floor and show an entire club her furburger.

Avoiding Hooking Up With a Friend's Family Members

If there is any event in the annals of Guido history that will always bring about unnecessary conflict, it's a guy hooking up with a friend's sister or other female relative. (NOTE: Needless to say, banging your friend's mom will probably precipitate some sort of armed nuclear conflict, so, uh, avoid that.) As you will undoubtedly find, Guidos have a strong protective streak when it comes to their sisters, especially if they are younger, despite overwhelming evidence that they aren't exactly choir girls who stay home on a Saturday night. That being said, you must not do anything to rock the foundations of this completely unrealistic image of a friend's sister, allowing her to be thought of as an angelic entity who just happens to share the phone number with the "for a good time" girl you were referred to in your local restroom.

These situations can be even more difficult if the girl in question is the one who is forcing the action. In many cases, a young girl who has constantly lived under the totalitarian glare of her older brother will purposely act out and try to rebel in an effort to test her given limits and constraints. This can spell bad news for you and, to a lesser degree, your penis. The best thing to do in this sort of scenario is to make a big scene out of rejecting her in a very public venue, preferably in front of her brother. This will help ease any potential tension between you and him, or at least delay the inevitable fracas. This is important, since his little sister will probably find you when you're alone and go down on you. Cue the fireworks.

"Just Friends"

It's assumed that, in general, there is a dearth of cross-gender friendships (between heterosexuals) as they almost always end in sweaty, awkward sex. While there is substantial anecdotal evidence to prove this theory, there are also scores of successful male-female friendships that provide a lifetime of care, support, and goodwill. These situations take on two shapes: (1) either one or both of the participants in this friendship are unfathomably ugly; or (2) one of the participants will have a not-so-secret crush on the other that will be exploited by said other for a great deal of material gain and inflated self-esteem. Let's be honest: in the mercantile world of self-worth and happiness, the only way you can improve your lot in life is to callously steal that of others. Nevertheless, from time to time you will still see these curious symbiotic relationships crop up at the Shore.

In the case of either you or your potential friend being just hideous to look at, it's probably for the best that you don't start wading into each other's gene pools. Think of the children. Despite the potential for carnal interaction in this case, it's quite apparent that two people devoid of sexual attraction can still be valuable friends to each other. (NOTE: Hey, it's worked for John Travolta and Kelly Preston all these years.) Budding friendships in this case are known for their ability to concentrate on "learning about your friend's interests" and "developing a personality that doesn't involve a blood alcohol content of 0.2." It may sound foreign, but having someone from another gender available is vital when you need a shoulder to lean on, or really need to talk out the difficult shit. That, and you'll still probably be able to get some sloppy, drunken sex out of it.

The other possible option for these peculiar cross-gender friendships typically occurs when Friend A has clearly developed feelings for Friend B, but Friend B is unwilling to reciprocate. You may recognize this as the plot from every John Hughes movie ever. In these cases, the hopeless romantic will always convince themselves that the romantic interest will someday see the light, stop dating douchebags or skanks, and come running into their arms ready to feel the eternal warmth of true and undying love. In real life, this never happens (sorry, Molly Ringwald). It's just an immutable law of human nature, like salmon swimming upstream, the sun rising in the east and setting in the west, and the fact that San Francisco will never, ever have a good sports bar. Needless to say, most of the time the guy or gal getting strung along finally figures out that waiting for a Guido or Guidette to see the light is a process that may span two or three generations, and will move on with their lives. The other unfortunate souls? They work at the tollbooths on the New Jersey Turnpike.

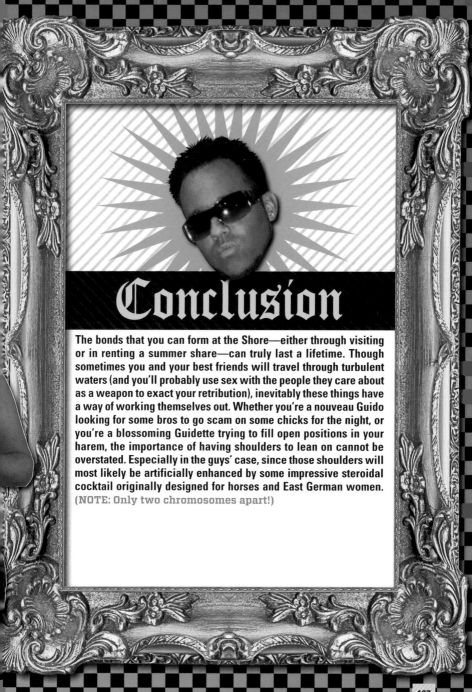

Conclusion

The bonds that you can form at the Shore—either through visiting or in renting a summer share—can truly last a lifetime. Though sometimes you and your best friends will travel through turbulent waters (and you'll probably use sex with the people they care about as a weapon to exact your retribution), inevitably these things have a way of working themselves out. Whether you're a nouveau Guido looking for some bros to go scam on some chicks for the night, or you're a blossoming Guidette trying to fill open positions in your harem, the importance of having shoulders to lean on cannot be overstated. Especially in the guys' case, since those shoulders will most likely be artificially enhanced by some impressive steroidal cocktail originally designed for horses and East German women. (NOTE: Only two chromosomes apart!)

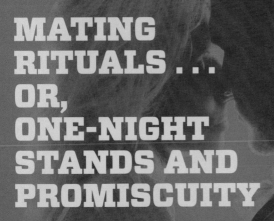

MATING RITUALS . . . OR, ONE-NIGHT STANDS AND PROMISCUITY

Just because you've crafted a killer body, know your way around the kitchen, and have assembled a small army of Guido clones doesn't mean you came to the Shore to spend time flying solo. And you probably could not have chosen a better place to sow your wild oats. Given the sexual proclivities of this region, it is actually somewhat shocking that Nathan's Hot Dog Eating Contest is not held here every year instead of at Coney Island, as there are probably at least three or four Guidettes you know who could give the Japanese dude a run for his money. Keeping this in mind, the quest for sex and romantic fulfillment runs at a fever pitch at the Shore, so you need to know how to prepare yourself for battle.

Men in Pursuit of Women

For a single man ascending into the Valhalla that is the Jersey Shore, life could scarcely be better. You are about to enter a world in which men and women wear their promiscuity like merit badges, and you can engage in activities that would make the cast of *Boogie Nights* blush. Oh, and did we mention there are hot tubs? They're like . . . everywhere. Some have even been cleaned since the Reagan Administration! This personal Candyland will allow you to spread your wings, spread some legs, and make a number of potentially life-altering decisions in an indecently short period of time. If you play your cards right and follow several simple steps, you'll be able to land so many skanks that Tiger Woods would tip his cap and wag his putter. (NOTE: That was not intended to be a sexual euphemism.)

As you start your night on the prowl, it's important that you lean heavily on your wingmen to fan out and acquaint themselves with the talent the club has to offer. If you see no immediate targets of interest, then it's quickly to the bar for a short reconnaissance discussion following some sort of shot that involves vodka, whiskey, and turpentine. After that, you just lather, rinse, and repeat until you've found a woman who will give you the

Members of the Opposite Gender You Would Have Sex with While Sober

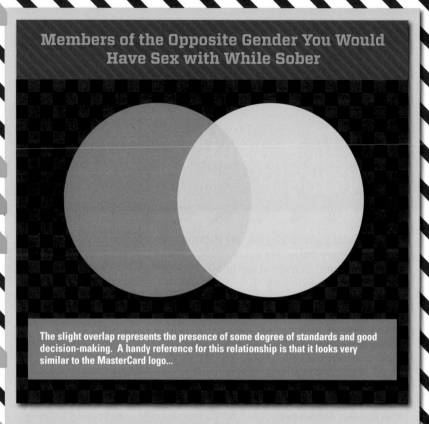

The slight overlap represents the presence of some degree of standards and good decision-making. A handy reference for this relationship is that it looks very similar to the MasterCard logo...

time of day. It's recommended that you try out a steady stream of lines until you find something that will work for you. There will certainly be times when you have been overserved to the point where speaking coherently is difficult, so it is recommended at this stage that you just take a deep breath, lift up your shirt, and point at your abs. Sadly, this will probably be the most compelling thing you say all night.

In some instances, you may not have had the best run of luck with the girls, but that doesn't mean you necessarily have to go home empty-handed. You need to learn to channel your inner lion and quickly identify the weak members of the female herd, ready to be taken down. Often, these women will make themselves easily known via broken heels or torn clothing, though smeared lipstick is usually a dead giveaway as well. If your target looks as though she is on the cusp of throwing up, but still will keep it all together, you've found your sweet spot. Proceed with caution, however, because she probably totally booted earlier, and that shit takes forever to scrub out of your soles.

On the other side of the coin, on some nights your mental faculties may be somewhat compromised, given the potent cocktail of Red Bull, hard liquor, and illegal Mexican horse steroids you regularly consume. There is a fairly high probability that this sort of devil's brew will lead you to make a decision some may call "curious," others may call "questionable," and the majority of folks would call "dreadful, potentially scarring, and probably illegal in thirty-eight states." We speak of course about the potential of hooking up with women who may be slightly below your typical standards.

If you find yourself consistently bringing home such women, maybe you should take a good hard look at your standards. Most men in other communities employ some sort of rating system when it comes to women, often assigning each one a number between one and ten for boneability. This sort of complicated numerical technique is only designed to savagely assault your sense of self-esteem if you tend to consistently bring home "lesser talent" as it were. In order to avoid this potential pitfall, we advocate a binary system that grades women as either "doable" or "not doable." This cuts right to the core of what you will generally value in your assessment anyway, and you may find yourself pleasantly surprised by the sheer volume of women in the first category (especially while inebriated).

Despite the pitfalls that litter the path you tread as a single, red-white-and-green-blooded American male, sporadically you will find a way to actually hook up with a girl who doesn't make you dry-heave. Finding a

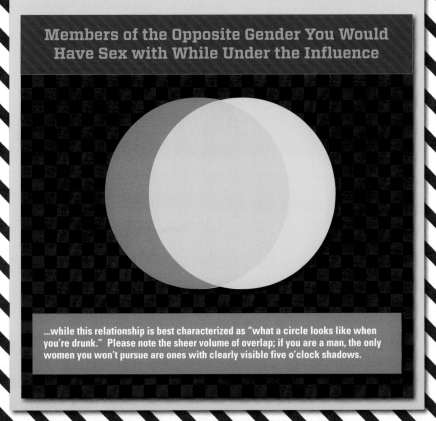

Members of the Opposite Gender You Would Have Sex with While Under the Influence

...while this relationship is best characterized as "what a circle looks like when you're drunk." Please note the sheer volume of overlap; if you are a man, the only women you won't pursue are ones with clearly visible five o'clock shadows.

beautiful woman who doesn't immediately whip out her pepper spray may be somewhat jarring to you if you've been wading in the swamp for a while, so to speak. Finding an attractive Guidette you can get along with (meaning she doesn't snap her gum so loudly that it shakes loose any of the drywall in your apartment) is the goal of every guy who comes to the Shore with only a gleam in his eye and the rhinestone-encrusted shirt on his back. Though most only intend to find a fuck-buddy for the short period of time they pass through this small sandy stretch, occasionally some will fall prey to the rarest of all diseases on the Shore: love.

Women in Pursuit of Men

As you single ladies survey the dating pool, you may find it a little more shallow than you had hoped (or you may think that some of your potential mates have been drinking the chlorine). It's completely natural to feel that way, and you should take solace in the fact that being highly selective will help guarantee that you won't settle. Though you may be inclined to succumb to the clever dick-related humor (undoubtedly referring to his virility and/or package size) offered by the first juicehead you see, it's important to take your time and see what's out there. This sort of clear, level-headed mindset is unfortunately a rarity, but by adopting this stance, you will be far more likely to avoid all the potential landmines.

Christy

555-1234

Hitting the club can be somewhat of a blur, so it's important to keep your wits about you and not let the amount of alcohol you are pouring down your gullet affect your faculties too much. Maintaining at least a baseline level of self-control will allow you to distinguish between a Russell Crowe and a Russell Simmons. There will come many times when you run into men who are so aggressive and annoying that your only recourse is to give them a fake number. If that's the case, you just have to run with it and never look back. Why not have a little fun with it? You'd be surprised how few guys notice that your cell number ends in 1-2-3-4. If anything, they'll probably just be surprised that your number ends the same way as the combination to their luggage.

Other guys who approach you may be a little subtler about their intent, trying to leave a little to your imagination. Some guys will even "slow play" so much that they'll try to add you as a friend on Facebook first. They may remark that they would "like to get to know you a little better" first, or some other hocus-pocus to cause you to let your guard down. Guidettes, you should know better. It's clear that this is just a cunning ruse on the part of a male to Facebook-stalk you and surreptitiously masturbate to several of your more scantily clad photos. Hey, it's not like we're telling you anything you don't already know. At the very least, that means that as an act of retribution you can start finding friends of his online and get stuffed more than a Chipotle burrito. Turnabout is, after all, fair play.

If you and your Whore Armada are able to wade through this desperate cesspool of undatable freaks, you may just find the Guido of your dreams occupying a space at the bar. The sunglasses on indoors, more jewelry than the three a.m. programming on QVC, a blowout that could stop a rhino at ten paces—The Total Package. Though you may be tempted to mount him right in the bar, such actions are generally considered a tad unbecoming and desperate. Your best bet is to play it cool and to flirt with this potential beau before allowing yourself to be coaxed out on the dance floor. At that point, he'll probably proceed to grind you so hard that you may notice some third-degree burns around your pelvic region. And with that, another seed of Jersey love will sprout.

Unbelievable as it may seem, occasionally you will run into couples whose relationships actually blossomed on the Jersey Shore. Rarely do you see a pair of people overcome a set of more impossible odds; it would be like the FreeCreditReport.com guys becoming the most successful band in America. Typically, the first three or four months of a Guido love connection are a curious mixture of rampant sex, cheesy fifth-grade-style dates (NOTE: let's just say you may need a Frequent Putter's card at the local mini golf course), and, well, rampant sex. Like your mama's meat sauce, it may not have a lot of ingredients, but you can tell when it's something you like.

Guidos, when it comes to planning your dates, it's important to notice your surroundings. Having a girl come with you to the gym may give her a glimpse of your natural habitat, but at the same time, she probably won't be much use as a spotter. Similarly, going to the tanning salon is an option, but only if you want her to see your skin with its disgusting natural tone of melanin. (NOTE: That's not even something you make her aware of by the six-month mark.) So, it's important to come up with a variety of options for the types of events and places to which you will be squiring your fair maiden around. Dinner at local Italian joints (though the Olive Garden's endless-salad-and-breadstick meal is a tempting option) will provide you with an air of authenticity and allow you to begin to get to know each other over her favorite tortellini. At the Shore, you have a variety of other options to start building your rapport—long walks on the boardwalk, intimate conversations in the aerial tramway over Seaside Heights, and walking arm in arm through the carnival as you both suck down arsenic-laden corn dogs.

An important part of ensuring that you have a happy Guidette on your hands is to buy her nice things to make her feel like she's well taken care of. Sure, you can go the route of just giving her whatever oversized stuffed

animal you've won from the basketball pop-a-shot on the boardwalk, but after a while she will probably run out of space for the twelfth Barney the Dinosaur. Your best option in this case is some high-end jewelry from a classy place like Tiffany's, where you can easily spend more money than your car costs. (NOTE: Though since it's a 1987 Trans-Am, that's not that impressive.) In order to really stretch the value of your dollar, you should become very familiar with the suffix "-plated." It can deliver all the punch of a great gift without so much of the hangover. If this is even a little out of your price range, perhaps you can purchase some jewelry out of one of those coin-operated machines you see as you're leaving the grocery store. It's always good to have options. As for you, Guidettes, there's only one thing you need to give your Guidos consistently through the relationship. Head. That's pretty much it.

Relationship Dynamics

Keeping the lines of communication open is a vital necessity in a Guido-Guidette tryst, given how quickly interactions can devolve into grunts, yelling, and hair-pulling (by both parties). With so many relationships resulting from what might have been, at one time, purely physical chemistry, many couples have to make things up as they go along in order to truly listen to what the other person is saying. Leveraging a wide variety of nicknames for each other is also a very common practice. Beyond the classically trite names like "baby" and "honey," though, you'll also occasionally run into guys calling their girlfriends "bro." This is a unique facet of some Guidos, who apparently can forget all rules of societal conditioning in how to appropriately refer to the sexes. This typically happens only when the male in the relationship is highly

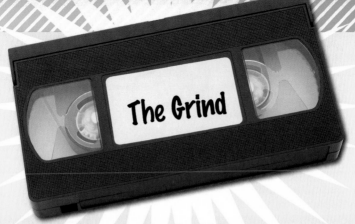

The Grind

intoxicated, so as you can imagine, it's a fairly regular occurrence on the boardwalk. It's also widely assumed that if your significant other refers to him- or herself by a self-given, narcissistic, over-the-top nom de guerre, you will refer to them by said nickname, if only to keep their unrealistically inflated ego sky-high.

In an effort to maintain consistent contact with your significant other, there are a variety of technological means that have shaped the way we communicate as a society. Whether you're using e-mail or Twitter or your cell phone, talking to someone you care about is suddenly at the touch of your fingertips, especially texting. While things can potentially get out of control and you could end up opening Pandora's box (NOTE: again, not a sexual euphemism, it's actually a commonly used expression), there's nothing wrong with a little flirting and being a little textually active. It's still important to try to maintain some sense of decorum while using your cell phone, though. Just because you think "sexting" would be a cute way for you to send your girlfriend a picture of your dong doesn't mean that it won't someday be used against you. It's pretty safe to say that every Guidette who ever sent a picture of her boobs to her then-lover has seen that photo careen around the World Wide Web approximately three million times.

There may be times in your relationship that you feel you've hit a rut. After all, eating pasta every night and sharing a glass of grappa as you play an old VHS of MTV's *The Grind* can get a little stale after a while. Yes, even if there's garlic bread. To inject a little bit of life into the proceedings, you may try injecting a little technology into the bedroom. That's right . . . it's the sex tape! This sort of calculated decision helped rocket the careers of Paris Hilton and Screech from "D-level talents" to "C-level talents who've done a homemade sex tape," and it could help you add some more fuel to your fire. Not only will you have the opportunity to really get down and dirty with your partner, but you can always watch it afterward and identify things that you'd like to work on or elements you'd like to add to keep things fresh. It's like you're a football coach, just with tits and ass. At the very least, you'll be able to give your homemade movie a kick-ass name. Leading candidates include *My Guzzlin' Vinny* and *The Cockfather* (or *The Cockfather, Part Tool*).

Like Adults

As in any relationship, there will be times when you and your mate do not see eye to eye. This is an especially significant issue at the Jersey Shore, since wanton steroid abuse and frequent drinking until you wake up in a gutter are pervasive problems. These scenarios clearly put more of an onus on you to make a persuasive argument to your partner in order to try to reach a resolution, or at the very least, grease the skids for some solid hate sex.

The first critical element to every Guido/Guidette argument is a distinct overreliance on childish name-calling. You are definitely going to want to belittle your partner as much as possible in an effort to break their spirit and make them realize that arguing with you won't actually get them anywhere. Resorting to this tactic may take you back to junior high school, but that doesn't mean it's wrong. You certainly also want to bring up past arguments and causes of discord that are unrelated to your current problem, as that will not be at all constructive and will add to a growing litany of resentment. You can't almost spell "sentiment without resentment." Finally, in every fight that you and your loved one have, you always want to make sure to engage in withering, vicious personal attacks at any lull in the conversation. Doing so will really start to chip away at the false construct of self-esteem they've been relying on, and will make your makeup sex all the more awkward and stilted. Fun times!

The Break-Up

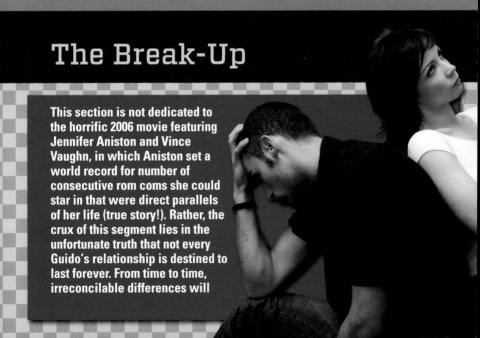

This section is not dedicated to the horrific 2006 movie featuring Jennifer Aniston and Vince Vaughn, in which Aniston set a world record for number of consecutive rom coms she could star in that were direct parallels of her life (true story!). Rather, the crux of this segment lies in the unfortunate truth that not every Guido's relationship is destined to last forever. From time to time, irreconcilable differences will develop, leading one or both parties to realize that they would be happier apart than together. While this sort of tragedy can be commonplace, such rational decision-making will unfortunately deprive the world of seeing what sort of freakish orange child you and your mate could produce. (NOTE: Most scientific studies estimate that the amount of melanin in the skin would be somewhere between a bottle of Fanta and a resident of Three Mile Island.) Keeping all of this in mind, though, there is definitely a right way and a wrong way to break-up with someone.

Many break-ups at the Shore happen as a result of purported instances of promiscuity or other instances involving sexual liberties taken by one partner. Occasionally, though, the mere *perception* of impropriety can get the ball rolling on a particularly vicious argument. You will find this is the case with any woman who claims to have a platonic male friend. Most guys find this as irritating as a college student returning from a semester in London who has to interject the word "mates" into every conversation. If you or your significant other cannot get around the roadblock that is infidelity, it's important to articulate your concerns in a constructive manner. This means minimal swearing and hopefully a distinct lack of sharp objects in your immediate vicinity. With any luck, you two should be able to cordially part ways and start ruining other peoples' lives.

There may be times, though, when your significant other fundamentally disagrees with this process, even considering your well-reasoned argument and the PowerPoint presentation that highlighted this sense of incompatibility. At this point, your focus should really just be on getting your shit back. Every tub of creatine you've left at her place (or alternatively, every tube of bronzer you've left at his place), is something else you'll have to waste your money on replacing. To say nothing of your Journey's *Greatest Hits* album. At some point, you just have to admit to yourself that some of your attempts at fostering an amicable separation may be futile, and cut your losses. If you, instead, turn your focus back toward winning every little argument, well, that usually ends up with people getting stabbed with nail clippers and a forthcoming date on *Judge Judy*.

Conclusion

Falling in and out of love at the Jersey Shore can happen in an instant. One moment, you're minding your own business, the next, you're going for the gold medal in synchronized fondling. With such a preponderance of young, nubile Guidos and Guidettes ready to cast common decency aside for a summer of decadence, there's no telling what can happen. There will certainly be times when you think you've found a Guido or Guidette who would make a good consistent hook up, then it just fizzles away for some reason. This is what happens when you live in a region that draws skanks and creeps like moths to a flame. If you manage to hit the jackpot and really find someone meaningful, though, you could find the person you were meant to be with. And at that point, you can start planning your wedding in front of The Taj in Atlantic City, and determining whether or not you can get bridesmaids' dresses in fuchsia for less than $75.

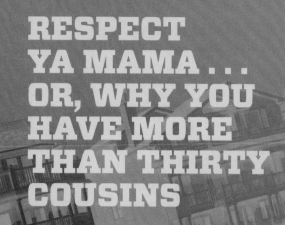

RESPECT YA MAMA ... OR, WHY YOU HAVE MORE THAN THIRTY COUSINS

Much about the Guido way of life is a product of learned behaviors and traditions. From the way you first learn all the ins and outs of colanders and Parmesan cheese to saying grace before consuming something as simple as a Tic Tac, the way you conduct yourself is a reflection not only of your family upbringing, but also of your community at large. Outsiders may not understand how a seemingly innocuous dinner invitation could potentially involve a larger ensemble cast than that of *Ocean's Thirteen*. These get-togethers will undoubtedly be seared into your long-term memory and retold countless times to professional therapists. All that being said, your family is a hand you're dealt at birth that you don't really have any say in; similarly to dating Chris Brown, sometimes you've just got to roll with the punches (too soon?).

Respecting Your Heritage

In order to help insulate yourself from the slings and arrows of potential adversaries who may question your Guido credentials, it's essential that you start to learn enough about Italian history to enable you to field any inquiries. While you may not initially know the difference between Frank Sinatra and Frank Stallone, some basic Internet research using Wikipedia should help provide you with a baseline understanding of the most critical facts. (NOTE: This could prove challenging, if, like a majority of Guidos, you are still reliant on Prodigy to log onto your 24.4 kilobaud modem.) You don't have to sound like a Rhodes scholar; all you're really shooting for is enough to get by. It should be easy enough to remember that the country looks like a boot in mid-kick, highly similar to one of your feet while engaged in a particularly fervent fist-pumping session.

Developing some degree of background knowledge on the largest cities, history, and current sociopolitical landscape of Italy is a good building block for your knowledge base. This will eventually come in handy when you are asked for your critique on the economic pros and cons of the shift from the lira to the euro. (NOTE: OK, this is about as likely as Kevin Federline winning an Oscar, but fortune favors the prepared.) Establishing an intricate understanding of the major exports and economic factors that drive the country is also a highly preferred custom. This means reading up on the regions of Sicily that produce the best grapes for fermentation, as well as determining which model of Fiat will manage to function for four months before falling apart and being sold as scrap metal.

You can also expand this to include cultural icons who hail from Italy, which will allow you to read up on accomplished personalities like Mario Andretti, Sophia Loren, and that super old broad from *The Golden Girls*. If you have the time, it may even be a good practice to learn some of the classic pieces of Italian music. That means brushing up on the Sinatra songs with the words you don't understand (we recommend

"O sole mio") as well as some of the classical masters of the old country like Rossini and Verdi. It's probably a good time for us also to mention that simply watching the dinner scene from *Lady and the Tramp* is not going to give you the cultural background you're looking for, unless you're planning on hitting on grade-schoolers.

Honoring Thy Pops and Thy Mama

As anyone who has ever watched *The Wonder Years* can attest, the father-son and father-daughter dynamic in a family is truly a sight to behold. How you get along with your pops is really shaped by a host of factors, such as how his relationship was with his father or how the Jets are doing this year. Males will find, in many cases, that they grow up to be the spitting images of their fathers, which means that the cast-iron potbelly that has been forged from years of drinking cheap domestic beer is a sad flickering harbinger of your future. Unfortunately, many Guidos have difficulty keeping their fist pump going past their mid-thirties. It's a fairly serious affliction that occurs from over-pumping before bones and joints develop properly, called *premature acceleration*. It affects approximately 30 percent of New Jersey men throughout their lifetime, and is the subject of at least two Bruce Springsteen songs. In addition, you will probably find that, much like your father, your mama has passed her prime as a Guidette. Though it's sad, time marches on. You just need to take solace in the fact that despite your mom's hardened, weather-beaten exterior, with a perm straight out of *Dynasty* and such a chain-smoking habit that Joe

Camel's penis face would start to lose its erection, she's still the envy of three out of five Atlantic City lounge singers.

Though these families may not spin the conventional wisdom on parental dynamics completely on its head, the matriarch possesses a vast array of power within the Guido household. It's assumed that beyond cooking every one of your meals, ironing your clothes, and sewing the days of the week into your underwear, your mama will help form an impenetrable cocoon around her children that will leave them impervious to pain (except that which is administered by a splintered wooden spatula). You may be inclined to say that your mom is overprotective and is afraid to let you live your life, but she looks over your grades and can probably tell that you are the type of person who would otherwise fall for a Nigerian e-mail scam within minutes of leaving the house. (NOTE: Though in your defense, that story regarding the deposed prince was fairly airtight.)

Beyond the mere fact that your parents will form an indelible imprint on your life growing up, it's essential to recognize that they may also occupy another important role in your life as you grow older: landlord. Yes, it's a fact of life for many Guidos and Guidettes that while you may see friends from other sectors start to leave the nest once they reach the age of eighteen or so, you may decide to dig your roots even further. After all, you're getting three square meals a day, have your bed made for you, and are only hassled by your mom 431 times a day about when you're going to get married and start crapping out grandkids for her. At any rate, you'll set the stage for some solid passive-aggressive prodding for the foreseeable future, all for the low, low price of free (plus your dignity). This whole scenario will still work for your mom, though, given that despite having thousands of meals under her belt, she still has not managed to grasp the concept of appropriate portion sizes and requires you to perform the role of food trough.

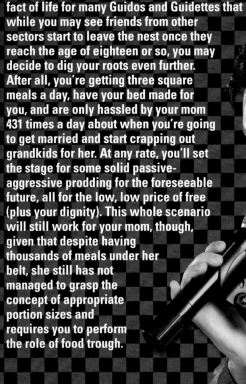

It's assumed that you spent a great deal of your childhood surrounded by a cavalcade of restless siblings; in many instances, your family was

probably mistaken for a youth soccer team. This creates a unique dynamic where you constantly have to battle with a cacophony of voices to become the center of attention, or fight to the death over the best scraps of mutton (ideally the high-protein shards). While this sort of dog-eat-dog mentality can be difficult for some children to thrive in, it also forces you to be highly self-reliant and constantly on your toes.

If you are not fortunate enough to have been born into a large family with multiple brothers and sisters for you to play with, it's not the end of the world. It just means that your parents don't love you. Or, at the very least, that the prospect of raising another demon spawn caused them to pour themselves a drink and read over the pamphlet on irreversible vasectomies. Regardless of whether kids are only children, this can be a potentially difficult time in the life of a child if he or she feels like they don't have an outlet. To that end, you might have been the type of kid to develop an imaginary friend, a fictional entity onto whom you could project your hopes and innermost desires, who would let you be yourself and would never turn their back on you. Man . . . that's just sad.

Growing up, tensions may begin to rise as the kids in a house hit puberty. This is the time in a family's life when relationship boundaries are tested, Stridex pads are consumed, and jokes about vaginas form the core of three in every four conversations. It's a wild ride. Things get even more complicated as these teenagers start to bring home prospective boyfriends or girlfriends. Guidos, it is written in your DNA that you must constantly threaten any potential beau for one of your sisters, either via actual delivered verbal intimidation or by menacing sideways glances that may make him wonder whether you've drained his brake fluid for the drive home. Whether or not you ever make good on those threats is your decision; it's expected that if your sister eventually marries the unfortunate schlub, you two will continue for decades an uncomfortable silence that will make every holiday dinner a delight. Not to be outdone, surely your father will do his best to ostracize this interloper as well, so that the males in your family present a unified front.

As for the Guidettes, though, it's just bad form. It's expected that you will continue to hit on your brother's friends despite the consistent beatings he promises them were they to act on your provocative suggestions. This is partially to increase the tension and strife in your family, but also because you never really forgave your brother for replacing your tampons with sidewalk chalk in the ninth grade (how the electric yellow color did not tip you off is still a mystery). As you grow older, though, you will begin to realize that families offer a great sense of comfort and are also a tremendous source of potential income just sitting there to be borrowed and never repaid. Beyond the mere hope of financial gain, though, it's good to know that you can always count on a roof over your head as well. (NOTE: It's estimated that after turning thirty, Guidos and Guidettes spend approximately two months of every year sleeping on pullout couches owned by their siblings, typically citing "termite fumigation" and "that damned direct deposit foul-up".)

Surviving in a Large Extended Family

It's probably no secret to you at this point that the makeup of the households we are discussing tends to skew toward not just quality, but quantity as well. Simply put, when Guidettes decide they are ready to have a family, they tend to be as fertile as the rolling plains of Iowa. This helps to create vibrant, growing family networks, though this level of productivity can also be burdensome at times. (NOTE: This is probably the only time in your life you'll be referred to as a productive member of society, so drink it in.) **This means that you'll probably have enough aunts, nephews, and second cousins so that your family tree will look like a Bernie Madoff pyramid scheme or the Cash Money Millionaires label.** (NOTE: Perhaps you could be Lil' Gwee Doh. There really aren't any rules for this sort of thing.)

A young Guido's formative years tend to be spent in the company of a bunch of male relatives around the same age. This helps establish a good group of kids who will either administer or be on the receiving end of an ass-kicking in your defense. You will probably notice in this environment that all of your cousins tend to have similar-sounding names; they may start to sound like Santa's reindeer. Additionally, if you look at standard naming conventions for male first names in your fast-developing Guido family—Johnny, Pauly, Vinny, Tony—you'll notice that pretty much every name ends with "y." This is due to a rather obscure tenet of the Guido civil code and can explain why no one named Arthur or Xavier has set foot on the Shore for at least fifteen years.

Growing up with a plethora of cousins is a good foothold when you're young, because it gives you someone to get into trouble with, as well as a convenient scapegoat that your mom will never press too hard on since there are family ramifications. As you start to slowly get on in years, though, you'll find out that going to the bars at the Shore represents a potential minefield in terms of the types of Guidos or Guidettes you may find yourself attracted to. Frankly, you're probably related to the lion's share of guys and girls you meet at the club; the chance you may run into a third cousin twice removed on the dance floor is fairly high, so you must tread carefully. It's at this point that you may start asking yourself deep philosophical questions like "How badly will this estrange me from my family?" and "Does *To Catch a Predator* have any sort of syndication royalties?" At this point, you need to just high-tail it out of there, maybe say a few rosaries, and take a cold shower for approximately two hours. Hey, it works for the Osmonds.

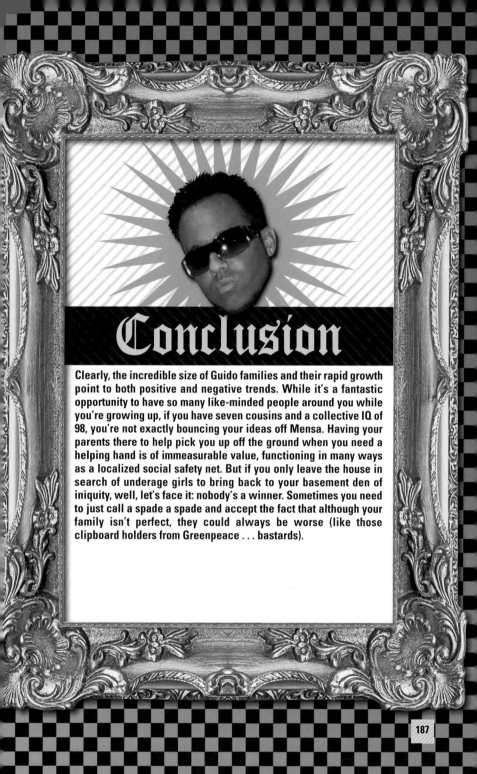

Conclusion

Clearly, the incredible size of Guido families and their rapid growth point to both positive and negative trends. While it's a fantastic opportunity to have so many like-minded people around you while you're growing up, if you have seven cousins and a collective IQ of 98, you're not exactly bouncing your ideas off Mensa. Having your parents there to help pick you up off the ground when you need a helping hand is of immeasurable value, functioning in many ways as a localized social safety net. But if you only leave the house in search of underage girls to bring back to your basement den of iniquity, well, let's face it: nobody's a winner. Sometimes you need to just call a spade a spade and accept the fact that although your family isn't perfect, they could always be worse (like those clipboard holders from Greenpeace . . . bastards).

PART III:
Lifestyles of the Juiced and Infamous

GUIDOS
AFTER
DARK
(UNCE . . .
UNCE . . .
UNCE . . .)

Though you may develop parts of your personality and body that you do not find immediately necessary, the value of improving all of these separate facets of yourself will be truly apparent once you decide to hit the town. Your knowledge of how to carefully concoct a delicious elixir of alcohol and energy drink will allow you to slowly lose your faculties, yet still stay up for the course of an entire evening. Cultivating the appropriate attitude of panache will ensure that while

new

SUGAR BOMB

MAHIMUM CC

at these nightspots, you are engaging in salacious contact with the opposite sex (and may even lead to several bad decisions!). You'll find that all of these items coalesce once you and your friends are ready to go out after dark and embrace the Shore for all it's worth.

Hitting the Bars

You may be somewhat apprehensive about coming to the Shore and immediately laying waste to whichever club you can get into. If this is the case (which would be very un-Guido of you), it's not the end of the world. If you'd like to get a taste of the nightlife in your city without paying a cover or waiting in line, you can check out a couple of your local watering holes. This will enable you to do a preliminary survey of the scene while concurrently slaking your body's unquenchable thirst for alcohol.

Your first order of business when checking out the bar scene in your particular nook of the Shore is to determine how much of a sausage fest it is. Whether or not it will be one is not up for debate; it's really just a matter of degree. If any female patron has been in said bar within the past calendar year, you should take it as a sign that you were meant to make this your own version of *Cheers*. If you can find one that also has an Irish-sounding name and has a salty bartender who's never met a bottle of Jameson he didn't try to crawl to the bottom of, you should just accept it as kismet and see if they have cots available.

If you are lucky enough to find a string of dive bars that don't smell so much like stale beer that they are constant targets for the Board of Health, it's up to you and your friends to do what any horde of irresponsible Guidos or Guidettes would do: pub crawl! All you need is a unifying theme so you can all dress alike (NOTE: more than the congruency you already display on a daily basis), **and a predetermined list of which bars to descend upon and overstay your welcome.** (NOTE: Tipping your local hospitals and drunk tanks is generally a nice gesture as well.) **Beyond just providing your whole group of friends with a set path to take and introduction to some seedy establishments they may not have previously had the pleasure of knowing, you may even be able to weasel your way into some drink specials. If you're at a bar that has suddenly opened its doors to the Trojan Horse that is a Guidopalooza, you definitely want to emphasize how affordably their newfound clientele can black out.**

Nightclubs

While the bars offer a great opportunity to bullshit with your friends and drink in a fairly low-key environment, you didn't come to the Shore to hole up in some booth watching a Knicks game. You could have stayed back in Piscataway in your mom's basement and done that. No, the truly hottest places to be throughout the boardwalk are always the nightclubs.

When it comes to finding the perfect nightclub, you're looking for one in which space is utilized as effectively as possible. At least 90 percent of available space should be dedicated to the dance floor, DJ booth, speakers, and associated sound equipment. Though this means you will probably have one bathroom for each sex to deal with the throngs of patrons you've decided to flout fire code for, it's assumed that most

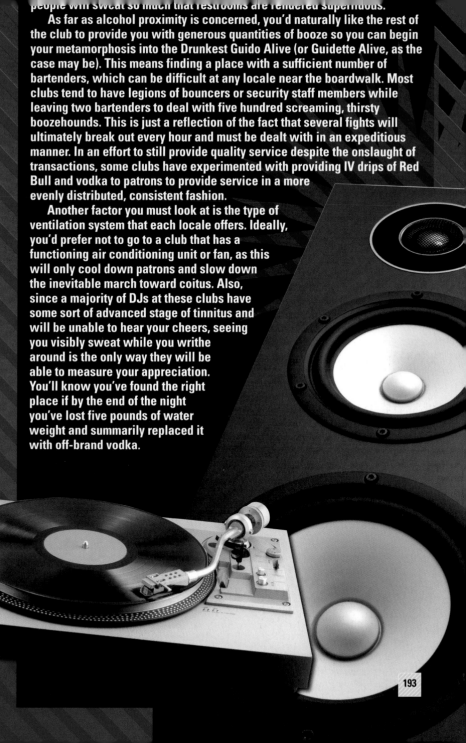

people will sweat so much that restrooms are rendered superfluous.

As far as alcohol proximity is concerned, you'd naturally like the rest of the club to provide you with generous quantities of booze so you can begin your metamorphosis into the Drunkest Guido Alive (or Guidette Alive, as the case may be). This means finding a place with a sufficient number of bartenders, which can be difficult at any locale near the boardwalk. Most clubs tend to have legions of bouncers or security staff members while leaving two bartenders to deal with five hundred screaming, thirsty boozehounds. This is just a reflection of the fact that several fights will ultimately break out every hour and must be dealt with in an expeditious manner. In an effort to still provide quality service despite the onslaught of transactions, some clubs have experimented with providing IV drips of Red Bull and vodka to patrons to provide service in a more evenly distributed, consistent fashion.

Another factor you must look at is the type of ventilation system that each locale offers. Ideally, you'd prefer not to go to a club that has a functioning air conditioning unit or fan, as this will only cool down patrons and slow down the inevitable march toward coitus. Also, since a majority of DJs at these clubs have some sort of advanced stage of tinnitus and will be unable to hear your cheers, seeing you visibly sweat while you writhe around is the only way they will be able to measure your appreciation. You'll know you've found the right place if by the end of the night you've lost five pounds of water weight and summarily replaced it with off-brand vodka.

BAMBOO BAR (SEASIDE HEIGHTS):

Perhaps the most famous of all Jersey Shore clubs, this place's reputation precedes it. PROS: best place to get your dance moves into high gear; smells like Axe Body Spray. CONS: can be difficult to get a drink, smells like Axe Body Spray.

JENK'S (POINT PLEASANT BEACH):

Located right on the boardwalk, Jenk's has been a mainstay for aspiring Guidos in the PPB area for years. PROS: good drink specials; great opportunity to see local DJs. CONS: close to the ocean so there is a good chance you may drown if overserved.

BEACH BAR (SEASIDE HEIGHTS):

Somewhat more laid-back (in Jersey Shore terms) bar if that's what you're in the mood for; more of a bar and grill. PROS: incredibly hot wait staff; good selection of drinks. CONS: fist-pumping opportunities are minimal compared to the club scene.

KARMA (SEASIDE HEIGHTS):

Karma is a staple for out-of-towners as well as locals, with an incredible atmosphere that keeps the party going both indoors and outside. PROS: great music, atmosphere, and bar staff who work hard. CONS: fist-pumping may get too over-exuberant, so you may be forced to sign a liability waiver.

PROVIDENCE (ATLANTIC CITY):

One of the foremost clubs in Atlantic City, Providence provides a steady dose of hardcore beats for true music aficionados. PROS: great atmosphere; always crowded. CONS: floor may actually be made of human sweat; is in Atlantic City.

The Ins and Outs of Appropriate Behavior

When you're out at one of these establishments, it may be difficult to get a sense of what behavior is appropriate and what actions are frowned upon by management. For instance, while Bamboo Bar may have no problem with a troupe of Guidettes dancing on tables, the same cannot be said for every place you'll encounter. Once you've been at your particular summer share for a couple of days, you'll probably have a decent lay of the land and be able to handle yourself in a suitable manner, regardless of situation. But as you'll see, there will still be times every so often when you'll do something untoward, so it's important to prepare for those instances.

What is probably the worst-kept secret on earth (except for Tom Cruise . . . c'mon, man, you're not fooling anybody) is that occasionally bartenders will violate their responsibilities and pour too liberally for their unsuspecting patrons. Drinking too much is an inevitability given that you will find a variety of locations that will literally set your alcohol on fire. Seriously, how are you supposed to resist that sort of temptation? At any rate, it's not about determining whether you've had too much to drink (you have), but where you are in the Hierarchy of Shitfacedness.

If you are somewhere to the left of the dotted line, that probably means you haven't begun exposing yourself or confessing your innermost secrets yet. Unfortunately, this means you will probably keep consuming until you've hit the point of no return. However, wherever you find yourself on this chart, you probably won't be officially asked to leave until you drop your pants or are seen expelling the contents of your stomach, given that bouncers will undoubtedly be concentrating their attention on breaking up the dozens of fights that are predictably occurring.

Regrettably, the presence of high quantities of alcohol will often lead to men or women being too laissez-faire in terms of hand placement on the dance floor or while at the bar. It's important to note that if you and a partner you have known for approximately seven minutes are engaging in a full-on grope session in full view of an assortment of spectators, you may be asked to leave before the entire bar is forced to witness the point of conception. (NOTE: Despite the relaxed rules enforced at most clubs, it's generally assumed that most folks don't want to watch you slip one past the goalie.) And that point assumes that your interest in one another is consensual; if you're getting a little handsy with someone who doesn't appreciate your advances, chances are that you will probably receive some sort of swift kick to the genitals as retribution. (NOTE: This applies only to Guidos; only in rare circumstances will a man stop a random girl—regardless of quality—from fondling his balls—incest and recuperation from testicle surgery being the only exceptions.)

After years of anecdotal evidence, it's unclear whether any clubs at the Shore have ever had issues with dress codes. The fact that some women will enter the clubs with clothing that can liberally be referred to as "full body condoms" probably leads you to believe that any possible statutes won't be enforced (NOTE: though the no-vulva policy is a strict tenet that all nightspots must abide by). Regardless, it's probably a good idea for the Guidettes to bring a couple of nipple pasties (or tassels) just in case the bouncer has a problem with your areolas. But don't get too fanatical about covering up; if you can't show your tits at some point, the terrorists have won. For the guys, your adopting a "no cock in public" mantra will most likely be appreciated by all patrons, and will minimize your potential for dick sprains and testicle ruptures. Let's be frank: the less said about showing your wedding tackle in public, the better.

HIERARCHY OF SHITFACEDNESS

SOBER

BUZZED

TIPSY

TOASTED

DRUNK

TIPPING POINT/POINT OF NO RETURN

FADED

HAMMERED

BOMBED

TANKED

WASTED / WRECKED / SHITFACED

DESTROYED / ANNIHILATED / OBLITERATED

CLINICALLY DEAD

Late Night Options

Sadly, there comes a time during every night out when you have to recognize that it's late and start to review the options available to you. Given that on many hard-partying nights, you will barely be able to communicate with anyone, relying solely on blinks and head nodding,

perhaps preselecting a variety of drunk food options is a wise decision. Pizza is always a classic go-to, given that there are a bevy of pizza joints dotting the boardwalk. An important characteristic of such an establishment is your complete lack of knowledge whether the food is good or not (or even fit for human consumption), given that your dalliance with their food typically takes place between three and five a.m. It's safe to say that it's probably not the best food in the world after each slice has spent more time under a heat lamp than Tara Reid, but the fact that you are still alive should be encouraging. Finding small carts on the boardwalk that specialize in "street meat" is also a necessity, given that eating a bacon-wrapped hot dog when you are drunk is the closest thing to heaven on earth that doesn't involve barbiturates and a massage parlor.

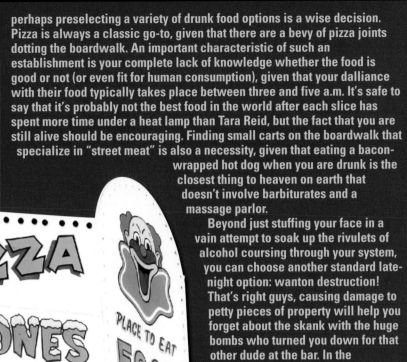

Beyond just stuffing your face in a vain attempt to soak up the rivulets of alcohol coursing through your system, you can choose another standard late-night option: wanton destruction! That's right guys, causing damage to petty pieces of property will help you forget about the skank with the huge bombs who turned you down for that other dude at the bar. In the communities of the Jersey Shore, this pervasive attitude has guaranteed that every mailbox and street sign installed since 1978 has had to be replaced at least once. This appetite for destruction is not only evident when it comes to trivial items, however. When you're properly annihilated is also a great time to spew endless amounts of venom regarding all the things in life that are bothering you, especially when the vitriol is directed at your friends and loved ones. This is a totally constructive process and definitely won't make everyone you're friends with think you're a huge asshole.

Every once in a while, you'll go paint the town red, yet still have the wherewithal to keep it together as the evening drags on. When this is the case, it's time to fire up the jets in your hot tub in celebration. There are a few rules of etiquette when it comes to the Jacuzzi, some regarding your attire and others that encompass your treatment of the venue itself. Guidos, you are expected to wear some variety of boardshorts upon entering the welcoming warm waters. **(NOTE: Disrobing during a hot tub session is expected and encouraged.)** Guidettes are expected to bring with them a bikini of microscopic proportions, though if you are going to the tub straight after the clubs, entering in your bra and panties is also totally acceptable **(NOTE: or one or the other, given the circumstances).** Regarding hot tub maintenance, it is vital that you apply some sort of standard daily cleaning cycle, or unequivocally you will end up with the hottest swamp north of Louisiana. Making sure to add twice the recommended daily amount of chlorine will help kill most of the icky stuff that grows in there, though you may want to add liberal doses of Valtrex as well. Providing pamphlets for tub-goers like "How to Live with Hepatitis" or "Herpes . . . So Now What?" is a nice touch, but not required.

How to Live with

Herpes

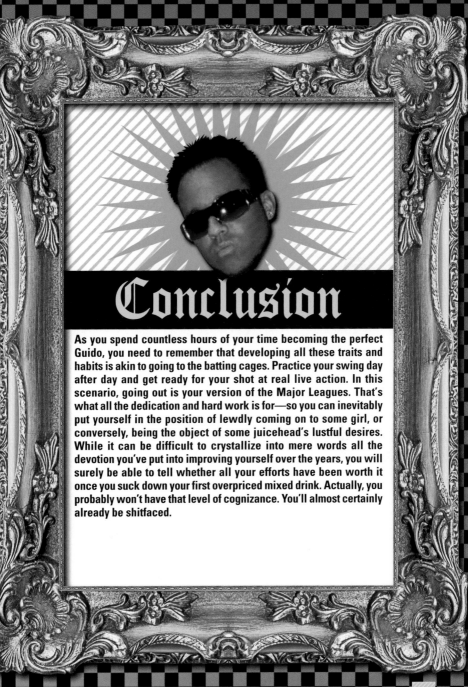

Conclusion

As you spend countless hours of your time becoming the perfect Guido, you need to remember that developing all these traits and habits is akin to going to the batting cages. Practice your swing day after day and get ready for your shot at real live action. In this scenario, going out is your version of the Major Leagues. That's what all the dedication and hard work is for—so you can inevitably put yourself in the position of lewdly coming on to some girl, or conversely, being the object of some juicehead's lustful desires. While it can be difficult to crystallize into mere words all the devotion you've put into improving yourself over the years, you will surely be able to tell whether all your efforts have been worth it once you suck down your first overpriced mixed drink. Actually, you probably won't have that level of cognizance. You'll almost certainly already be shitfaced.

FIST PUMP . . .
OR, OTHER ACCEPTABLE
FORMS OF DANCING

If there's anything that will help define your essential Guidotude, it's the ability to get into a club and just rip it up on the dance floor. We're talking about the ability to cast your inhibitions to the winds, forget about the three or four paternity tests that may be working their way through the New Jersey circuit court system, and really get after it. Fist-pumping. Hair-flipping. Occasionally, even, the worm. The artistry you choose to bring to the club really depends on how you want to paint, with the dance floor as your canvas. You can't just go out and start winging your fist around without an iota of training, however. In order to get out there and really make the guys and girls start picking up what you're putting down, you have to at least pretend to know what you're doing. Hell, Ryan Seacrest has made an entire career out of that.

Vital Pre-Dance Activities

Before you go to the club, a good use of your time (besides hammering down champagne flutes of Goldschläger) is making sure you've taken the appropriate measures in terms of stretching. Nothing's worse than getting yourself revved up for a sick fist-pumping session if you end up going out there and fracturing your patella during your first attempt at splits. There are a couple of helpful stretches that you'll really find invaluable when looking back at your routines in hindsight. First of all, you want to really focus on your groin muscles. Not only are these important for giving you the flexibility to actually execute your totally-not-derivative moves, but if you end up rocking it with the spotlight on you, there's a good chance you'll *really* be using those groin muscles later. (NOTE: We're referring to sex, in case the subtleties of italics are lost on you.) You also definitely want to make sure to do some deep knee bends or some hamstring stretches, as some of the dancing you'll be doing can get pretty demanding on your lower body. Finally, you certainly need to devote a healthy amount of time to your fist-pumping shoulder. Making sure you've got all the kinks worked out there could save you from a costly dislocation that could put you on the Jersey Shore sidelines for months. Just remember: no dude in a sling ever gets laid.

Let's be honest. While getting limber is a valuable step that will help ensure you don't tear an ACL or pull a hamstring, it doesn't really matter how loose you feel if you don't have the balls (or ovaries) to go after the moves on the dance floor. The quickest and most effective way to overcome any jitters you may have prior to your lurid gyrations is to saturate them with bottom-shelf, low-quality booze. Basically, if you can pass a field sobriety test, you're not ready to dance yet. Try saying the alphabet backward if you want a simple exercise to quiz yourself. (NOTE: If you cannot say the alphabet forward, please employ a different exercise.) We're not even talking about casually sipping a gin and tonic or throwing back a shot or two. We're talking about drinking HEAVILY, the type of drunk where dancing is a natural extension of your limbs rather than an act you have to willingly participate in. Once you've got enough booze sloshing around in your belly so that you can legally change your last name to Belushi, you'll be ready to let yourself go.

Fist-Pumping Basics

The best way to describe this dancing style would be to liken it to trying to jump and punch something two feet taller than you, while simultaneously moving your legs forward and back as if you were on a NordicTrack. If it sounds complicated, it's because it's an incredibly difficult maneuver. While it may sound impossible, it is actually much easier in practice. The main thing to remember is that your upper body and lower body will simultaneously perform different motions, yet they will appear to be in harmony. Regarding your legs, it's really just as simple as performing lunges while remaining in place, albeit at an incredibly high speed. The true masters of the floor have been able to gain such acclaim, not for the size of their biceps or fists, but rather because their footwork and agility have been developed to levels only previously seen in Tasmanian devils in cartoons or Kevin Bacon in *Footloose*.

Preparing your upper body for a true dance marathon is an entirely different proposition. If there's anything you need to know about the fist pump, it's that it's not just a one-off movement. Raising your fist like a gleaming beacon to the sky is a truly holy act, so just doing it once (and not repeatedly, to the detriment of your rotator cuff) is a grave insult to the Lords of the Dance (see Michael Flatley et al.). In order to be taken seriously as a Guido, you must prepare your fist to reach time and time again to the heavens, rather than making one meek thrust in the air as if you were at a Savage Garden concert.

There are two appropriate motions for the fist pump, which depend entirely on your lower body. If you are performing the recommended cross-country skiing maneuver, you should opt for a fist-pumping style that looks like you are preparing to spar a few rounds with Oscar De La Hoya. This means stiff, rigid arms that jab forward at an upward angle. You may have seen a similar type of punch by Ryu from Street Fighter II. If you are only shuffling your feet back and forth in place (again, this is not recommended; the odds are quite high you will look like a tool), you can pump your fist in a rotating manner. Though this may make you look like an audience member from the halcyon days of Arsenio Hall, at the very least you'll be fisting like crazy. (NOTE: There's got to be a better way to say that.)

One of the first things you should do upon entering a club is to take a comprehensive inventory of what sorts of amenities the dance floor provides. As Bruce Dickinson would say, you want to "really explore the studio space" regardless of how the club is laid out. This means taking a detailed scan of the room and seeing what items could potentially be utilized during the full-body convulsions you refer to as dancing. Virtually any item can be used to take your gyrations to the next level, like that column near the middle of the floor that's being used as a load-bearing support (and poorly, since the club probably has not been renovated since the Carter Administration). It's actually a world-class stripper pole, if used properly.

Guidettes, once you find the stanchion to your liking, you can opt for simply twirling around it like one of the third-rate strippers working the noon shift at the Eager Beaver that you aspire to be. The problem inherent with this, though, is that it's not unique. It's been done approximately a billion times at the Jersey Shore in the last seven years. Another inevitable issue with this move is that, with your clear level of intoxication, it's probably a foregone conclusion that you will lose your grip and careen off your makeshift pole into an unfortunate bunch of bar patrons. Instead, you should sidle up to your chosen column and start grinding the hell out of it like you were operating a floor buffer. This will allow you to really play up the idea that you are riding a giant phallus, and the crowd will appreciate this clever attention to detail.

It's also a good idea to map out the location of the speakers. Though the house music pulsating out of these monstrosities will undoubtedly be played at an unhealthy volume (most likely raised to the level of a jet engine or Fran Drescher's voice on *The Nanny*), you can start to view these speakers as potential adversaries. By standing right in the path of these brutal sound waves, you are asserting that you will not let the music beat you. If you want to bring it up a level, you can scream into the speaker as a way of fighting back when you're really feeling it. Not only will this allow you to channel a primal form of energy, but you'll look just like you're auditioning for every Michael Jackson video from the eighties.

Absurd Moves

If you've exhausted your entire repertoire of fist-pumping (and generally looking like an overcaffeinated child with ADHD), and the crowd is *still* not putty in your hands, it may be time to bring out the big guns. This nuclear option can definitely get out of hand quickly, but if you execute a couple of outrageous moves right off the bat, the throng of onlookers will be yours. This follows the old Guido adage: Anything is worth doing if it guarantees you will make a spectacle of yourself.

The easiest way to cause everyone else in attendance to freeze is to bust out the back flip. This combines all the things Guidos and Guidettes want from a dance move: risk, daring, and the undeniable possibility of seeing someone suffer a massive spinal injury. This move can usually be performed in one of two ways: either from a standing base or via a running start. If you're able to imitate the little Chinese dude from *Ocean's Eleven* and bust out a back flip with no momentum, then just go for it. People will be amazed to see a guy the size of a refrigerator demonstrate such an amazing semblance of agility (though realistically, the density of your muscles will probably not permit you the coordination to pull this off). If you require a running start, we recommend you start moving at a decent clip, and then utilize one of the walls near the dance floor as a springboard to launch yourself. If you can throw in a gainer or a triple axel while you're at it, your odds of going home with the classiest skank in the bar will go up exponentially.

Another item that should be in every Guido's bag of tricks is called the Guido frolic. This absurd series of dance steps will almost certainly earn you immediate notoriety, and could potentially lead to your ejection from the club if not carried out properly. This move is fairly basic, but much like the board game Othello, it takes a minute to learn and a lifetime to master (for Guidos, that statement also applies to long division). This move is executed by moving your feet very rapidly in a small square of space like you are playing *Dance Dance Revolution*. The only difference is, that, unlike DDR, if you pull off this move effectively, you at least have a chance of getting some ass. It is vital to maintain proper balance, though, since your hulking upper body may send you tumbling to the dance floor at a moment's notice. And once Guidos hit the deck, much like turtles, they have a very difficult time getting back up.

If, at this point, your narcissistic whims have still not been satiated, you can start to bust out old-school break-dancing moves like the headspin. We would advocate doing a variety of other moves, but frankly, the more time you spend on the floor, the more potential damage you're doing to your $100 plain white Armani Exchange t-shirt. Not only will the headspin manage to leave your clothing unscathed, but it's not like your skull is a valuable piece of property. Have at it, chief. If you have still failed to win over the crowd, we must suggest that you never opt for cheesier dances that will indisputably make you well known (albeit not for the right reasons). The Shore is no place to trot

out your updated take on the Charleston or bust out the Macarena, even ironically. (NOTE: It's a well-known fact that the concept of irony is lost on most Guidos.)

Guidettes are invited to perform all of the aforementioned dance steps to their hearts' delight. However, there is a move specific to the female sex that will always get hearts racing and cell phone cameras out in an instant. We speak of course of the cartwheel. This move can be executed properly only in the absence of undergarments so that your goodies are visible to everyone in attendance. It's also a fairly well known phenomenon that cartwheels, much like their fist pump brethren, never occur in nature as a solitary maneuver. This means that once you start a cartwheel, you'll probably end up doing around ten or twelve, to the appreciative cheers of your potentially horrified spectators, who will now probably be able to pick your nether regions out of a police line-up.

Music

Before you head to any club to start your evening of dance-related calisthenics, you should always do an extensive background check of the DJ who will be putting it down on the wheels of steel that night. Far too often, you'll end up at some place that plays only hip-hop, which may be fairly off-putting as you still can't comprehend the appeal of that Lil Wayne character. You should be trying to emphasize any club that has a preponderance of house and trance music at its disposal. As far as the DJ is concerned, basically anyone who's been to Ibiza besides the Vengaboys is an appropriate source for inspiration. (NOTE: If you do happen to take frequent trips on the Vengabus, it's probably time for you to step back and take an inventory of your life.)

Though many of your favorite DJs will most likely be the giants out of Europe—Tiësto, Ferry Corsten, basically any one with "Van" in their name—you will probably have to make do on the Shore with a variety of local characters who drip gel onto their Technics sets. It's just an unfortunate by-product of being a Guido. Though these guys may not have the worldwide cachet of some of the global music masters, they will undoubtedly know exactly what tracks to play to inspire a Guido frenzy. This means more fist-pumping, more cartwheels, and of course, more anonymous, casual sex.

Conclusion

While in other segments of the American population, dancing may be "a fun night out" or "a nice way to meet some new people," in the Guido culture it means so much more. It's a method of self-expression that also serves to provide males of the species with what may be their only form of cardiovascular exercise. It allows Guidettes an unfettered opportunity to demonstrate that while they may be dressed like skanks, well, gosh darn it, they can act like skanks, too. If you can master a handful of key moves and steps, you'll be well on your way to making an ass of yourself in the most efficient way possible.

GUIDOS LEAVING THEIR NATURAL HABITAT (THINK SPANIARDS MEET AZTECS)

While the Jersey Shore offers a veritable smorgasbord of opportunities for Guidos and Guidettes alike to get themselves into an unfathomable amount of trouble, occasionally it is a nice change of pace to visit some surrounding locales in an effort to gain some semblance of perspective. Guidos leaving their natural habitat can get into a variety of unforeseen problems and

211

potentially hilarious mishaps, mainly because the possibility for culture shock is so pronounced. For instance, you may find that some cities outside the cocoon that is the Shore lack the amenities you are used to, such as Axe Body Spray dispensers in the bathrooms of the clubs you may happen to frequent.

The interaction between Guidos and non-Guidos (hereafter referred to as Nuidos) offers a stunning glimpse into the sociological structures that these competing societies have built. Though these cultures have historically existed peacefully side by side, occasionally there have been brief eruptions that have threatened the prospects for Guido-Nuido tranquility along the eastern seaboard. Much like the Aztecs during the arrival of Cortes and the invading Spanish armies, it is important for Guidos to preserve their sense of culture and remain unspoiled. Though this desire for purity can occasionally manifest itself in a desire never to leave the comforting string of communities that make up the Shore, if you can develop an ability to look beyond your own borders, you'll be all the better for it.

Atlantic City

Occasionally, there will come a time when you want to feel the rush that comes with legalized gambling. Fortunately for those at the Jersey Shore, Atlantic City is a mere hop, skip, and jump from the madness that is beach life. To get a sense for what AC is like, imagine Las Vegas after some sort of nuclear fallout. It's essentially a poor man's Reno, which is already a poor man's Las Vegas. When one of the major features of your resort is that you accept U.S. currency, it's safe to say that you're probably a major shithole. That should give you some idea of the accommodations you will encounter. And once you venture away from the main strip, some of the hovels you will have the opportunity to stay at are truly astonishing; some parts of the city are gritty enough to make characters from *The Wire* shit their pants.

Let's just say that Atlantic City leads the nation in "percentage of establishments that will happily rent you a room by the hour and/or still utilize quarter-operated massage beds." Sadly, AC ranks second in terms of "motel rooms that obviously were formerly crime scenes of a grisly murder" (but they're nipping at your heels, Trenton!).

Of course, the lure of Atlantic City is not just confined to walking a creaky boardwalk and getting viciously mugged. Clearly, this is a worldwide mecca for degenerate gamblers who can't afford a flight to Vegas or the drive to the Indian casinos up in Connecticut. These dregs of society contribute mightily to Atlantic City's bottom line, since other avenues of tourism have been somewhat stunted. (NOTE: In the city's defense, it's difficult to create a marketing slogan that rhymes with "garbage dump.") Many Guidos and Guidettes will ignore the potentially long odds of making money at the tables on the off chance that they may stand to make it big. Sure, having the mathematical education of a precocious second-grader won't help you play the percentages appropriately, but then again, you won't have the intelligence to know when you're facing a hopeless situation.

It's true that AC does offer a little bit of something for everyone. Guidettes will love the clubs because they are slightly different from the Karmas and Bamboo Bars of the world, and at the very least, you'll have a whole new host of men willing to feel you up inappropriately. Guidos will certainly appreciate these new watering holes and the new faces therein, but there is another appealing aspect of this city, especially for the man who has been on a little bit of a cold streak: hookers. While some may view this as a last resort or tantamount to just giving up, you need to really own this experience and celebrate it for what it is. How often do you get to choose exactly where you'll be parking your cock for the evening? Not only that, but you will simultaneously be celebrating the virtues of capitalism while taking your lovely date on a one-way trip to Poundtown, U.S.A.

Lake Parties

Curiously enough, when many Guidos decide they want to get away from it all and see another part of Jersey, they often travel in droves to lake parties to get hammered and dance on boats, effectively recreating their Sodom and Gomorrah slightly inland. It's almost as if there is a DNA pair specific to the Guido species that makes members want to party harder than the larger body of water around them. Unfortunately, many Guidos do not adjust their behavior to fit a newfound situation, so you often get a fair amount of hard-core fist-pumping and frolicking on the slippery surfaces of many a fiberglass boat. Tragically, this has led to the drowning of dozens of Guidos and Guidettes over the last decade, contributing to a 2 percent increase in national IQ. To compound the potential peril of these situations, this is the only place in America you will probably see frequent usage of stand-up Jet Skis, which are only slightly less dangerous than sitting shotgun with Stevie Wonder or the No. 3 Combo Meal from Taco Bell.

If you are undaunted and still wish to get your party on, lake-style, more power to you. The first thing you have to do before leaving for your lake of choice is to secure a boat (though this should be obvious to everyone, it's surprising how many folks forget this item). You should be able to find several places near the lake in question where you can rent a kick-ass powerboat with limited background checks. This will help to obscure your obviously bad credit and help the boat rental companies go out of business at a much quicker rate. You can obviously also borrow a boat from a family member if your dad/stepdad/brother/uncle has made the incredibly unwise decision to invest thousands of dollars in a vessel that will only drive him batshit crazy. Seriously, do you have any idea how hard it is to find a good barnacle-removal place these days?

When you actually get to the lake, it's essential to find an existing group of Guidos who have established a stronghold position at the lake and tie up with them. Once you can get four or five boats tied together, your potential

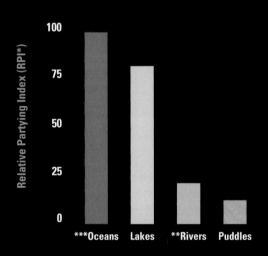

Relationship of Guido Partying vs. Bodies of Water

Relative Partying Index (RPI*)

***Oceans Lakes **Rivers Puddles

*The Relative Partying Index (RPI) is calibrated as follows: a score of 0 equates to a book club meeting in a library while a score of 100 is equal to an open bar in Ibiza.
**Also includes babbling brooks, streams, rivulets, creeks, tributaries, and the occasional isthmus.
***Access to the Atlantic Ocean explains the ridiculousness of the Jersey Shore party scene, though it should be noted that the partying apex for a Guido would be alone on an ice float in the Arctic Circle with the newest Armand Van Buren mix.

Alcohol Usage vs. Sunscreen Misapplication*

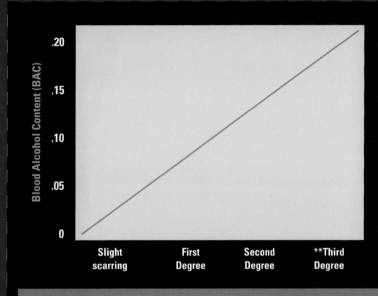

Blood Alcohol Content (BAC)

.20
.15
.10
.05
0

Slight scarring | First Degree | Second Degree | **Third Degree

Severity of Burn

*Typically, the forgetfulness of the subject to reapply sunscreen increases at a fairly linear rate when viewed next to the subject's alcohol intake.

**It's entirely possible that if BAC wandered into a potentially fatal territory of .30 or higher that the subject might look like Wesley Snipes in *Passenger 57* afterward.

for drunkenness, sunburns, and lewd behavior will rise exponentially. As soon as you've established a critical mass, the good times will inevitably ensue. If there's one inevitable trait of a lake party, it's that your typical predilection for hard alcohol will shift to cheap canned beer. This is due to the fact that carrying handles of hard alcohol can be cumbersome, and dropping a handle of shitty tequila into the depths would be a tragedy, while cans of beer will float and generally function as highly portable units of liver destruction. In order to really maximize your fun on the lake, you must remember to follow the old rule of thumb that the further into the blackout you get, the more likely you are to forget to apply appropriate volumes of sunscreen, which will enable everyone back at the Shore to estimate how awesome a time you had.

New York

If you are looking to go to a city that's less sketchy than Atlantic City (basically if you're looking to go to any other city), you'll find that NYC is not too distant from the Shore and can provide you with limitless options. This vibrant mecca for tourists throughout the world is well known for having a variety of different flavors and experiences that can be tailored to your personal tastes. For instance, if you have really been dying to see the latest David Mamet play to hit Broadway, a good set of orchestra seats could be well within your grasp. (NOTE: Let's be honest, though, the odds of that happening are more remote than David Hasselhoff getting an Emmy nomination.) What is probably more realistic is that you'll end up going to some club that's open till six a.m., striking out hardcore with the ladies, and getting into a fight with a homeless guy who takes issue with your liberal interpretation of public-urination statutes.

If you are looking for a place that will be most accommodating to Guidos, Staten Island is probably your best bet. This borough has the highest scumbags per capita rate in all of New York City, which should provide you with all the joys of visiting a new place, while still offering you the feeling of never having left your summer share. You may find that the pseudo-Guidos in this borough are very similar to the folks you would traditionally interact with back in Wildwood or Long Branch, but the more frequent your interactions, the more disparities you will see. The clearest example is that residents of New York City tend to value their tans far less than does the typical Guido or Guidette, which contributes to an overwhelming fog of pale (in fact, the pervasive lack of any dark skin pigmentation may cause you to draw parallels to the 2008 Republican National Convention). You will also notice that these folks may want to discuss world issues or burning topics of the day. Feel free to make fun of these people, and then quickly switch the topic to more important things, like the value of squat thrusts.

The Hamptons

Once in a great while, you may end up taking a severely wrong turn and end up in a particularly tony area of Long Island. Once you've seen P. Diddy's fourth estate, you'll know what we're talking about. The Hamptons are a collection of expensive houses, clubs, and galas that draw a collection of the rich and famous year after year. In many ways, their draw during the summer parallels that of the Jersey Shore, except that the visitors tend to be "successful" or "wealthy" as opposed to "likely to be charged with some form of public lewdness." This fundamental disconnect is a source of potential misunderstanding, so at the very least, you should bring a translator with you or pick up a pocket guide to Guido-prick communication.

Should you and your Guido friends attempt to stay out in the Hamptons for any extended period of time, you will most likely feel like an outsider looking in. Try as you may, your system of distilling the entire world population into either "bros" or "broads" runs the risk of potentially not being understood by the upper stratum of society. (NOTE: If you are having any difficulties envisioning this scenario, just imagine some sort of Guido version of *The Beverly Hillbillies* or *King Ralph*.) You will be able to recognize your status as a fish out of water pretty clearly as soon as some asshole at a party goes on a meandering diatribe about some article he read in The Atlantic on the slow-food movement. The only appropriate way to respond to this sort of interaction is to deliver a merciless beating, get back in your Pontiac, and make that fateful trip back to the boardwalk.

Other Locales

As for other parts of the U.S., it is unclear whether Guidos have ever left the tri-state area. Years of anecdotal evidence would lead one to conclude that the farthest west Guidos have ever traveled is the Mystic Tan in Wilmington, Delaware. Regarding international travel, that is an even bleaker portrait. As of this publication, zero passports had ever been issued to Guidos, depriving our brothers and sisters in Africa, Europe, and South America of the glory that is the blowout.

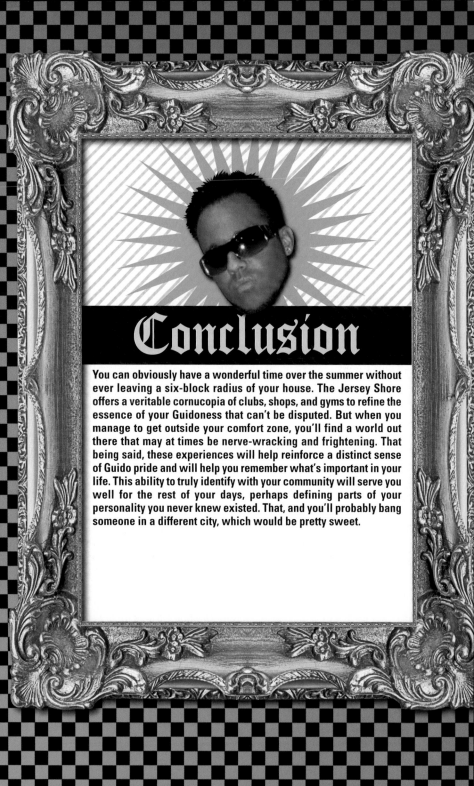

Conclusion

You can obviously have a wonderful time over the summer without ever leaving a six-block radius of your house. The Jersey Shore offers a veritable cornucopia of clubs, shops, and gyms to refine the essence of your Guidoness that can't be disputed. But when you manage to get outside your comfort zone, you'll find a world out there that may at times be nerve-wracking and frightening. That being said, these experiences will help reinforce a distinct sense of Guido pride and will help you remember what's important in your life. This ability to truly identify with your community will serve you well for the rest of your days, perhaps defining parts of your personality you never knew existed. That, and you'll probably bang someone in a different city, which would be pretty sweet.

DENOUEMENT

We hope this book has demonstrated some vital areas of import that will help you truly fulfill your destiny as a Guido or Guidette. If you didn't find every section valuable, that's understandable, given that you probably read three-quarters of this tome while perched on the toilet. Regardless of where you decided to consume this useful guide, it's time to take these lessons that currently exist only as written word and turn them into valuable real-world applications.

The body is your temple. As you incorporate these lessons into a daily ritual, you will begin to notice changes in your body (it's like puberty all over again!) and in the way you approach social situations. This means extensive work at the gym. But by spending countless hours lifting heavy weights and eating the proper foods, you can cultivate a lower body fat percentage than Lara Flynn Boyle after a bout with a tapeworm. Hitting the tanning salon in a consistent fashion will enable you to bring out a pumpkin hue that will really accentuate the work you've put into that body; after all, you don't lift weights for seven hours a day to look like you're auditioning for Vampire Weekend.

Furthermore, as you begin to assemble a clever fusion of mildly offensive tattoos, low-budget plastic surgeries, and uninspired clothing choices, you'll start to develop a fake sense of originality that you can apply as part of the smokescreen you refer to as your "personality." The crown on the entire persona is really the hairstyle you choose to address the world with. Crafting some spikes that would make the Statue of Liberty jealous lets any wayward onlooker know exactly what they're getting before accidentally meandering with you into a conversation. Harnessing all these physical traits together with an attitude that says you'd rather punch first and ask questions later will really add the icing to the cake.

It may sound like an exercise in futility to distill all that goes into a Guido into several obvious personality traits. Actually, though, it's pretty easy. Seriously, there is not much room among this community for individuality, so if you're ever in a jam, just go with the herd mentality. Doing so will help you assemble an army of friends in your own likeness, help you go after that guy or girl to your liking, and start building a family that will undoubtedly continue pumping out Guidos and Guidettes for years to come. It's a lot like Mormonism, except that you can have caffeine and you can travel outside of Utah. As you begin to raise children of your own, undoubtedly the more precocious ones will start to ask you questions about what is right, what is wrong, and what choices they should make in life to be successful. That's the time for you to take them aside, smile wistfully, and suggest that a drive to the Jersey Shore may provide some guidance as they grow up in these turbulent times. Ah, and the cycle begins anew.

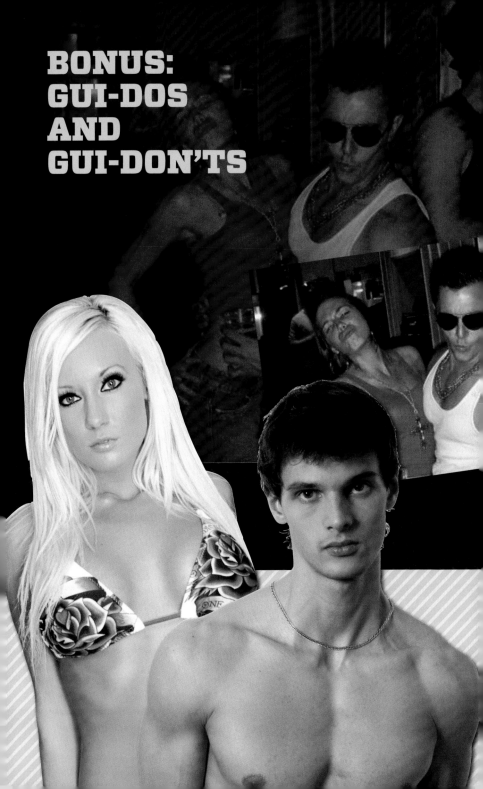

BONUS: GUI-DOS AND GUI-DON'TS

Gui-dos

COOKING SPAGHETTI WITH MEAT SAUCE

ROTTWEILERS

CHIHUAHUAS

GIANT TUBS OF HAIR GEL

FIST-PUMPING

HIPPY ATTITUDES TOWARD FREE LOVE AND SEX

TONY'S PIZZA SHACK

BUYING GOLD JEWELRY

HIGH HEELS

SPENDING MONEY

LOOKING GREAT

ANY MOVIE WITH AL PACINO

HANGING OUT IN A POOL

GRADUATING FROM BARTENDER'S SCHOOL

KEEPING YOUR LONG ISLAND ACCENT WHEN YOU RELOCATE

BOOB JOBS

SKETCHY MYSPACE PICTURES

ENHANCED HOME-RUN HITTING BARRY BONDS

CADILLAC

BUMPING STEREO SYSTEMS

SCARFACE

DOING THE DISHES

SCHNAUZERS

OLLIES

HAIR PRODUCTS FROM TRADER JOE'S

DOING THE ROBOT

HIPPIES

CALIFORNIA PIZZA KITCHEN

INVESTING IN GOLD ON THE STOCK MARKET

COMFORTABLE HEELS

EARNING MONEY

BEING HEALTHY

ANY MOVIE WITH JOHN CUSACK

SWIMMING LAPS

GRADUATING WITH A PH.D. IN CHEMISTRY

PRETENDING YOU HAVE A LONG ISLAND ACCENT AFTER ONE WEEK
ON LONG ISLAND

NINE-TO-FIVE JOBS

PRIVACY SETTINGS SO PEOPLE CAN'T SEE YOUR
SKETCHY PICTURES

ORIGINAL BASE-STEALING BARRY BONDS

KIA

FUNCTIONAL EAR DRUMS PAST FORTY DECIBELS

FACIAL SCARS

Big thanks to all of the loyal fans of guidofistpump.com. Who knew how big this Guido thing would get a few years later? Without all of the fun you guys bring by sending in great pictures and making hilarious jokes and comments, this book would have never come together. So thanks, and hey, if you're reading this and haven't been to guidofistpump.com, go check it out. And now the shout-outs. (NOTE: Imagine the last song on Sublime's *40oz. to Freedom* is playing in the background.)

Starting off—Jay Noskini, JJ & Tony Gardocki, The Cos, 9k guides and homies, Sean and Tommy, Goomba Mikey Agnello, The Britalian Raccoon, Tiny Delgado and Pete, the Gamma boys, West Side Ninja Poker Crew, David G. and the whole crew, you guys rock!, Bro, Rents, KK, and special thanks to ML, my ol' friend from the Holy Land, for the inspiration. Lastly, this thing never would have happened without the furious mind of my illustrious co-author Rick "The Happenstance" Marinara.

—Guido DiErio

Thanks to all of my friends and family who helped hone a personal desire to never be serious, and to look for the humor and irony in as many situations as possible. My parents deserve special thanks for letting me watch six hours of TV a day growing up for . . . umm . . . research purposes. Thanks to my Best Buds for always providing a forum for a witty, urbane comment (unlikely) or patently offensive remark (commonplace). Much appreciated, fellas. A special *domo arigato* to JL for the JL, or else this book would have never been finished. Finally, my heartfelt gratitude goes out to all of the coffee shop owners in "The City" who allowed me to occupy prime seating and filch their Internet for countless hours while only spending in the neighborhood of $5.87. (Except for you, Café International. I managed to drop a significant chunk of change your way, partly due to the friendly environs and partly because you have good beers on tap and don't look sideways at people who order a pint at eleven a.m. You're the best). Finally, thanks to Double E for helping pave the way for this. It's been a fun process, man. Keep pumping away (fist-pumping, that is . . . keep your head out of the gutter).

—Rick "The Happenstance" Marinara